Published in 2010 by

Responsive Solutions UK Ltd
Ziggurat Building
60-66 Saffron Hill
London EC1 8QX

www.responsivesolutions.org.uk

Email: jim@responsivesolutions.org.uk

A catalogue record of this book is available from the British Library.

ISBN 978-0-9564863-0-1

Design and Typesetting by Profile Communications, Bristol.
Email: pnorris@profile.u-net.com
Typeset in Minion and Myriad.

How Nurture Protects Children

Nurture and narrative in work with children, young people and families

By Jim Rose
M.A. (Cantab)

Responsive Solutions

Contents

Acknowledgements

How Nurture Protects Children - nurture and narrative in work with children, young people and families is a collaborative effort. The ideas and examples used throughout the book come from many years of working and talking with remarkable people; professional colleagues, including foster carers, as well as the children, young people and families whose stories are central to the purpose of the book.

I take full and sole responsibility for the opinions expressed in this book and for any errors that may be spotted. I offer no apologies for the strength of these opinions, but they are mine and mine alone.

With the above disclaimer, however, the final text would not have been possible without some very specific help.

John Reid provided wisdom and comments as the chapters emerged and Pat Williams, a distinguished former head teacher of a school for children with disabilities, undertook valuable research. Paula Sobieckowska also gave her time to talk through some important aspects of current social work training issues and was both insightful and helpful.

The Caspari Foundation, of which I am proud to be a Trustee, promotes and provides educational psychotherapy. Some of the material published in an article I wrote for the recent edition of their journal is included in extended form in chapter 4.

I am particularly grateful and indebted to the Nurture Group Network for permission to use Network sources and to Professor Tom Billington for providing me with access to material from the Evaluation of Nurture Groups Project. The Nurture Group Network is an innovative and creative organisation that promotes nurture groups with extraordinary vigour and is supported by the boundless energy of its many members. In particular I should like to thank the Network's Life President, Marion Bennathan, for her friendship and support over recent years.

During the past eight years The Fostering Foundation has given me many opportunities to meet with that very special group of people who look after needy children and young people in their own homes, namely foster carers. I offer them special appreciation along with the staff teams in our regional offices.

Paul Norris of Profile Communications has been extremely encouraging and helpful and it is due to his creative skill that the final design and printing are of such a very high standard.

Finally, to Jean, who is not only an experienced and skilled social worker but a true partner. She continued to believe in the book and to offer encouragement even when it seemed less than clear to me what road I should follow. I hope I have taken 'the one less travelled by' and for that I thank her.

Jim Rose
December 2009

PREFACE

How Nurture Protects Children is neither an academic textbook nor a research thesis. I have drawn upon the findings of research and hope that the arguments I have put forward are persuasive and intelligible. For the most part, however, I have relied on the sort of knowledge that comes from direct experience; in this case from work with children, young people and families in their homes, in schools, in foster homes and in residential settings over a period of many years. These are my experiences and the experiences of others as they have told them to me.

How Nurture Protects Children expresses the frustration of many who see the work that they are trying to do with vulnerable children, young people and families undermined by an overwhelming and dominant culture of procedures and protocols. In this world a day's work is measured in terms of outputs whilst thinking and reflection are considered of lesser value. However, in order to avoid any suspicion of 'grumpy old man' syndrome the book is unequivocal about the importance and effectiveness of thoughtful work that gives value to the unique stories that, irrespective of their age, all have people have to tell about their lives. These stories may be told in a class room, a social work office, a front room, a residential home or even a secure unit. *How Nurture Protects Children* is positive and hopeful about this sort of practice, offering models of thinking about how this may be done in ways that ascribe value to human relationships. The growth in our understanding about the crucial importance of good early attachment and nurturing experiences for healthy emotional development is now supported by increasing knowledge of how the infant brain grows and develops. This is a knowledge base that needs to be taken much more seriously in the formation of policy and in the education and training programmes of all those who work with children, young people and their families.

Robert Frost wrote that the true poet's pleasure is in '*making his own words as he goes.*' I make no claim to be a poet; However, I do want to make my own words about this very important subject. I do not expect you to agree with everything I have written. However, if the book makes you think a bit more or in a different way about the work that you do, then its purpose will have been achieved.

FOREWORD

We read with horror the stories that unfold in the press concerning violence and abuse, inevitably accompanied by 'blame' falling on someone who is accused of 'not doing their job.' It's as if we have no other way of dealing with this extreme end of the continuum of behaviour and relationships other than by blame, punishment and hysterical accusations of 'evil'. But there is a huge body of knowledge and experience which defies this notion. It is possible to 'make sense' of such behaviour, to understand the story behind the events, which in no way condones it or seeks to avoid responsibility for responding appropriately but informs how to intervene in a way which tries to remedy the harm done and minimise future occurrence - a pathway to a healthier society.

Those who work in the frontline of such outrages are very exposed to the powerful and often toxic feelings of the perpetrators - fear, rage, despair - and can become traumatised themselves unless they are protected emotionally by informed insight and protective supervision.

Those who set the guidelines for our care and protection, have long emphasised a practice of coping by measured outcomes and detailed recording - social services, policing and education are now built around a framework of measured outcomes using criteria which reflect little of the struggle that many vulnerable people express through their behaviour but are easily transformable into charts and graphs. It is almost as if managing the problems with protocols is a way of dealing with the anxiety they evoke.

In this timely book, Jim Rose examines how this way of coping has developed and the harm it can do relative to an approach which seeks to see behind events, creating more relevant and mentally healthier alternatives. He argues that the framework for understanding should be common to all social and educational professionals, which makes shared understanding possible and strengthens responses and the containment of the anxiety associated with such distressing events. In particular, vulnerable children can be identified early in the context of schools when such understanding is built into the training and support systems which at the moment, it is not, leaving many vulnerable young children at risk of disaffection and subsequent social exclusion. Jim argues that the current system of managing challenges by measuring the incidents and outcomes is not addressing the problem and must change to one which is shared, collaborative and supported by a common understanding of the causes.

Dr Heather Geddes
Educational Psychotherapist and Author

Introduction: Is it me?

'Science is a collection of stories about facts, not a mere collection of data dumps'

(Adam Gopnik)

In talking with friends and colleagues about my thoughts for this book, the rather grandiose notion that I might be alone in having concerns about the current and pervading culture in the professions of work with children, young people and their families was always quickly and sometimes rudely shattered! The ideas and the premise upon which *How Nurture Protects Children* was written found ready acceptance, although others still frequently expressed doubt that anyone else would be interested enough to publish such a book, or would give a hearing to such concerns. "It's a great idea, but do you think anyone will publish it?"

So what are these concerns about how we are working with our most vulnerable children, young people and families? Professional activity in social care, education, youth justice and health services has been dominated for a number of years by policy directives that require copious forms to be completed, papers to be filed, boxes to be ticked, targets to be achieved and reports to be written. The latter usually in a formulaic style, with their conclusions already prescribed and sometimes even with helpful, prepared phrases ready for cutting and pasting; 'Here's one I made earlier!'

Even with the supposedly more sophisticated systems, where paper forms are replaced by electronic recording, the problems remain the same. For if – according to Adam Gopnik (2009), with reference to the eighteenth-century astronomer William Herschel – 'science is a collection of stories about facts, not a mere collection of data dumps,' then we have some way to go before our systems and evidence-based approaches help professional workers avoid simply dumping data into endless bundles of electronic forms, and instead help them connect the facts before them with the stories behind them. Along with the demands made on all professional groups to be overly exercised about procedure and protocols, increasing constraints are being placed on the use of previously accepted concepts, such as professional judgement and the use of discretion in making decisions.

Short-term outcomes are the order of the day, with a requirement for focused pieces of work that can be written off and added to the list of jobs 'done' and performance measures achieved. The rationale for much of this is shrouded in the perceived importance of evidence-based approaches and a reliance on quasi-scientific methodologies to justify short-term interventions that also, conveniently, meet the need for being cost effective.

In practice, this has brought about a series of unintended consequences, most dramatically a number of high profile child-protection cases, which are routinely followed by a process of enquiry, reports and knee-jerk policy reactions – generally resulting in more of the same.

After so many enquiries and reports, it might be thought that social carers and other workers would be more aware of the risk factors that indicate a family is having problems or a child is suffering in an abusive situation. The reality is that front-line workers appear to have less understanding about the meaning of what they are seeing or hearing and are ill-equipped in terms of knowing how to ask the right questions and think about the answers.

This is the critique I shall explore in more detail in the following chapters. However, this book is only partly a censure of a culture in which control prevails over welfare, regulation prevails over professional judgement, and protocol prevails over process. It is also an attempt to describe alternative ways of thinking about work with children, young people and their families, irrespective of the setting or organisational context. In contrast to the current situation developing and sustaining positive relationships are at the forefront of policy and practice, whilst the education and training of professional workers is shaped by an emphasis on child development and on the profound significance of attachment and nurture.

CHALLENGING CURRENT THINKING

How *Nurture Protects Children* challenges the current thinking about the critical relationships between policy, practice, and training. It seeks to raise questions about how we speak about the work we do.

A recurring theme throughout this book is studying how language is used to express the thoughts and feelings generated by close, personal work with children, young people and their families. Work with children is undertaken by a host of different people, all of whom have varying experiences and backgrounds. It is important that a common framework of language is agreed upon to ensure that proper communication about complex or potentially life-threatening situations is possible. Amongst these groups, I make specific reference to foster carers, who are such a vital resource in the child-care system but rarely receive recognition as such. Finding ways of including them in conversations about risk and risk-management is critical.

As suggested above, one effect of the present culture is the inhibition of thinking. This may be partly ascribed to a lack of connection between the world of the professionals and the daily experiences in the lives of the children and families they are trying to engage. This gap is often widened by the use of 'professional' language (embodying a set of the professional values and beliefs) that seems alien or incomprehensible to many, and which only serves to confirm the imbalance of the power dynamic between workers and their disadvantaged clients.

Perhaps one of the most serious failures evident in current practice is the apparent inability of front-line professionals to hear the unfolding narratives of their clients' lived experiences – even after interacting with them over long periods of time. Other demands, usually of a bureaucratic nature, impinge on this process of listening. In recent years, the importance of narrative has been increasingly understood in therapeutic work, whilst the significance of telling stories has been acknowledged since the origins of language itself. Narrative methods not only provide options in therapeutic work, but are also useful for understanding aspects of the organisational process. In subsequent chapters, I shall try to show the relevance of narrative work for vulnerable children and families in the context of nurturing and attachment-focused approaches, as well as its relevance to organisational development and management.

TO PUBLISH OR NOT TO PUBLISH?

But back to the original question posed by my friends: 'Who do you think will publish this book?' Indeed, it might well be asked why this should even be an issue. Paradoxically, in seeking to answer this publishing question, I continued to find plenty of examples to illustrate one of the main tenets of the book –that thinking and critical reflection no longer appear to be requirements for those involved in practice, and seem to have only a minimal part to play for students on initial, qualifying training courses. Had I offered to write a 'how to' manual, offers might have come streaming into my in-box! As one publisher, in reply to my proposal for this book, wrote:

> In reaching this decision, [to not publish!!], we would like to say that
> we felt the idea of drawing attention to the need for the development
> of positive relationships and secure attachments as the keystone of
> policy, practice and training, is very valuable, and are equally sure
> that your central point about what is missed by a 'tick box culture' may
> well offer the key to what is actually going on in a particular client's
> life. We feel you are absolutely the right person to be writing this book
> along the lines you describe. However, we feel that the book would be

*fundamentally discursive in nature, more background/vision-based than offering hands-on strategies and interventions for practitioners ... **Our sense is that qualified practitioners, policy-makers and even trainees in the professions you mention are reading less and less 'around' the subject, wanting instead to find 'how to' material, grounded in and supported by accessible theory.** (my emphasis).*

Without being quite sure what 'accessible theory' is and putting aside any flattery about my credentials to write this book, the point is made and I accept it. I shall consider my writing discursive and vision based! Nevertheless, I also intend to be bold enough to challenge the conclusions of this particular publisher about what 'practitioners, policy-makers and even trainees' want. Over recent years, it has become clear to me (through discussions with not only friends and colleagues, but also in formal meetings, training sessions and conference presentations) that amongst experienced professional workers there is a widespread and deeply felt sense that there are real gaps in the knowledge base of newly qualified practitioners who are joining the workforce. There is also – encouragingly – a growing recognition that the way in which the practice is presently focused does not result in the provision of the best care and protection for those children and families most in need of it. In trying to engage with often very resistant children, young people or families, the stakes are high and there are really no neutral outcomes. The underlying worry is that this focus is having a corrosive and pervasive effect on the quality of the care and educational experiences offered to the most vulnerable groups in society.

In the arena of public debate, however, attempts to challenge the present status quo are all too often dismissed as 'old fashioned' or 'lacking an evidential basis'. A good example of this sort of dismissive attitude can be detected in the government's immediate response to the findings of the Cambridge Primary Review, a massive report into the state of primary education today. For daring to suggest that formal education should not start until children are six years old, that play-based approaches best support children's early learning, and that over-reliance on a central curriculum with a regimen of testing is counter-productive for improving children's attainments, the report was dismissed almost out-of-hand as 'disappointing and backward looking'.

This response by the government raises questions about what sort of material is likely to be taken seriously and viewed as sound evidence for the purposes of making policy, and it certainly introduces a clearly political dimension into discussions about evidence-based practice. The fact is, however, that even statistical data – usually regarded as the most credible form of evidence – seems increasingly compromised when it is used to answer such important questions as whether the educational attainments of looked-after children is rising, whether there are there fewer children at risk of significant harm, whether youth crime is reducing, and whether the general mental health of our young people is improving.

REFLECTIONS AND EXPERIENCE

In many respects, this book is a series of reflections on my own work and experience over the past 35 years. I have not attempted to write an academic thesis, but I have drawn upon some recent research projects that demonstrate the tide may be turning and that offer hope to countless number of managers and workers. These are professional people who know by experience that there are better ways of approaching their work, but they are not sure of the ground upon which to build that alternative. It is their experience, as well as my own, that I intend to validate and put to use in challenging the present way of doing things. This work is not tilting at imaginary windmills or being nostalgic for halcyon days that may never have been, but offers a serious and credible set of ideas and models to make things better for children, young people and their families.

The issues and problems in this book are relevant to almost every area of public life – not just to the welfare, justice and health-systems that are our immediate concern. My own career has extended from community youth-work in south London to managing residential work in both open and secure children's homes. I have worked as the national professional advisor to HM Prison Service with responsibility for advising on the placement and management of young people sentenced to long-term custody for the most serious of offences. I have managed social care provision for children and young people, chaired fostering panels, and supervised and trained staff in all of these settings. Most recently, I have been the executive director of a national voluntary agency, the Nurture Group Network, which gave me opportunities to visit dozens of schools across this country and overseas to see how nurture groups and allied models of practice really do make a difference, both to the lives of children and their families as well as to the ethos of whole schools and communities.

In an era when there is a premium on multi-agency work and the integration of services, it is even more essential that theoretical and practical models for engaging and supporting vulnerable children and young people are applied to different disciplines, and that they make sense to all professional workers. In this respect, foster carers deserve a special mention.

In recent years, foster carers have made an increasingly significant contribution to the care of children and young people, providing them with accommodation and support at what are usually difficult and disturbing times in their lives. The issues discussed throughout this book are especially pertinent to the situations that face foster carers, not only because of their perceived lowly status within the professional hierarchy (which is demonstrated whenever a case conference is convened), but in terms of their hugely important role as people who offer direct care. We shall explore in detail the difficulties and constraints that foster carers face in their work, and how their success at providing care depends on their ability to develop significant and direct relationships with children and young people.

STRUCTURE AND CONTENT

In chapters 1, 2 and 3, we focus on policy issues and the current context in which policy has been developed and consider the impact on managers and workers.

Chapter 1 considers what has been described as the 'split' that has emerged between knowledge and experience (Billington 2009). This is exemplified in the way that particular significance is ascribed to certain kinds of 'knowledge' and to so-called evidence based approaches to evaluation. Over-reliance on prescribed views about what constitute 'scientific' approaches is challenged, and a specific example from the Nurture Group Network shows how the use of narrative creates different and important perspectives for the purposes of evaluation.

The content of initial training programmes for workers at the start of their careers in teaching or in social work has changed dramatically over recent years, as has the culture of the higher-education sector within which they are taught. Pressure to increase student numbers has raised questions about the overall academic quality of the intake, whilst the modular design of courses and emphasis on skills and competencies has raised questions about intellectual rigour.

Whilst there are some advantages to integrating professional training across different disciplines, there may also be unintended negative consequences. Rather than improving the understanding of related areas of practice, the absence of an historical perspective within the training culture, and the continuing failure of training programmes to connect experience and learning perpetuate the existence of professional silos that prevent real engagement between different professional groups.

Policy-shifts, along with the increasingly bureaucratic nature of the tasks in practice settings and a demand for particular topics to be made priority in training programmes have resulted in a narrowing of the curriculum. The squeezing of the curriculum prevents sufficient space being created for students to gain experience in thinking and reflecting. Amongst all the skills deemed essential for practice, these are the crucial ones for work in areas of high risk or with vulnerable groups of people.

Chapter 2 is entitled '*Mind the Gap.*' Here, a gap is defined as '*an empty space between two objects*'; in this case, the empty spaces between professional workers and their attempts to engage with the daily, lived experiences of ordinary people. Those who create the policy framework establish the priorities that managers and workers must pursue, usually through targets, performance indicators and outcomes prescribed to measure success. There seems to be an underlying assumption that the more organised the systems (which often means more bureaucratic), the better will be the outcomes. No account is taken of the profound anxiety evoked in workers who must engage with vulnerable or delinquent people, which undoubtedly contributed to the poor decision making that was highlighted in recent high profile child protection cases.

The most commonly used formats for supervising workers tend to prioritise 'performance monitoring' and task completion. These are preferred to models that adopt a more holistic approach – those that take into account the individual worker's experience and reflect on what might lie behind the complex and often bewildering feelings generated through their relationship with the client. It is also noteworthy that there are some practitioners who do not work under any model of supervision, including teachers in mainstream services and prison officers who have responsibility for looking after more than two thousand young people on a daily basis in the juvenile estate.

Relationships are defined as '*dealings that exist between people*', which in the normal run of things would seem an apposite description of social work or teaching. Chapter 2 explores how relational models of human services successfully build the necessary bridges for crossing many of the identified gaps. These models prioritise qualities such as trust, and they value the common elements of our human experience whilst seeking to avoid both collusive practices and failures to confront difficult issues. To be effective, relational models of practice must be supported by robust and supportive management systems in which workers have regular access to highly skilled supervision and training.

Chapter 3 explores the paradox in which, alongside the strong policy lines for regulation and the imposed standards that have emanated from central government, there has been a different policy line associated with emotional awareness and well-being. This has served to create a conflict of agendas for managers, and the result is that performance and achievement are prioritised, whilst the implementation of nurturing practices and the development of nurturing environments is limited.

Considerable resources, including large amounts of money, have been put into health and education services to support the development of emotional awareness and to increase resilience in children. However, because of the prevailing policy context, those who are outside of the family but work in the practice settings in which these issues are perhaps best addressed (i.e. schools) feel they have no alternative but to employ methods for delivering the programmes that oblige them to reflect the central, overarching requirements of regulation, monitoring and reporting. Whilst there may be specific activities for 'teaching' self-esteem, raising emotional awareness and building resilience, there is widespread agreement that these cannot just be regarded as curriculum subjects. They must be properly developed in children and young people through the direct experience of positive relationships with the adults entrusted with their education and care.

In chapter 4, we see how nurture groups provide the outstanding model for offering children and young people a set of experiences that increases their self-esteem and builds up their resilience. Nurture groups have been well established in schools for over 40 years and have a sound theoretical base drawn from attachment theory and new findings in neuroscience. The conclusions of the main research projects show that nurture groups are both an effective and inclusive intervention that very successfully engage even the most vulnerable or troubled children and young people.

The principles of nurture groups provide an exciting template from which other services for families, children and young people should be encouraged to draw upon in fulfilling their particular duties and responsibilities. For this to happen, however, there must be radical changes in the mindsets that dominate how policies are formulated and in how managers in organisations respond to the task of ensuring their implementation through the delivery of services.

Chapter 5 examines some specific and contentious areas of professional practice and shows how those involved in direct work with children and young people have seen their practice reshaped in recent years by the priorities of policy, the demands of bureaucracy, and an increasing emphasis on risk assessment and management.

Entitled *'What do you do when there is nothing you can do?*, this chapter explores how the emphasis on targets has increased pressure on social workers, teachers, and youth justice and health workers to deliver quick results. The preference for managers is short-term pieces of work, tightly defined time frames, and a focus on presenting behaviours. There is no time for thinking or for building a therapeutic relationship within which the underlying causes of a child or young person's distress may be understood and addressed. Such short-term interventions, in what are often highly complex and long-standing circumstances, are at best limited and at worst dangerous, because they invariably prevent workers from gaining a broader perspective on a situation or being able to hear a story in terms of its 'beginnings and endings'.

The nature of the work is such that sometimes a story is so painful to hear it creates a sense of helplessness and hopelessness. Support for staff must include acknowledgement that it is essential to think about the meaning of difficult feelings, and that change takes place over time because effective work has to be undertaken within a framework of consistent and stable relationships. What have become commonplace events, such as changes in organisational structure, the introduction of endless 'new initiatives' and knee-jerk responses when a crisis occurs are all especially counterproductive when working to people bring about changes in their lives.

When a serious incident occurs, the existence of a culture of blame (rather than support with accountability) militates against the creation of safe working environments capable of containing the extreme anxiety that inevitably surrounds such 'hot' issues as child abuse or other forms of sexual violence.

Another important theme of this chapter is the examination of the crucial elements of work done by social care staff and foster carers, especially that which takes them into the personal space of vulnerable children and young people. The key daily routines that provide stability and containment for traumatised children in residential or foster homes inevitably involve adults having to enter bedrooms to wake children or settle them at night, or having to help them with intimate personal tasks such as washing and bathing.

These tasks all take place in what has become a widespread culture of risk aversion. Foster carers are advised to tell bedtime stories via a baby-alarm intercom, or to keep a pillow between them and a child seeking a cuddle. Teachers and learning support assistants are instructed not to have physical contact with a child who is in distress – even to the extent of not putting a band-aid on after the child has fallen over! Children need adults around them who are confident and responsive to their needs; preventing them from receiving this level of care may only serve to further damage the very children most in need of safe and comforting adult contact.

Risk and fear: what is their origin? And how can they be managed so that both children and adults feel safe and secure? What do they mean for foster carers who have to provide public care in the private space of their own homes?

Chapter 6 explores one of the frequently identified problems for current child protection practice: the failure of different professionals to connect their experiences of one family with the experiences of other professionals dealing with the same family at different times. A child who is seen at school, at home, or in a doctor's surgery may have a different story told about them (and what is thought to be happening in their life) following each visit. The report of a social worker visiting a family in their home captures only a snapshot of how things are (or seem to be) at that moment, and this limited view is emphasised by a tick-box style record of the visit and its outcomes. If a social worker fails to make any links with their report and those from previous visits, or between their experiences and those of others who may have visited in a different capacity, then disaster looms. Similarly, if there are frequent changes of workers visiting a family, then there will be no continuing threads with which to weave a more detailed narrative.

Thinking in narrative form allows different voices to emerge. Everyone's story is relevant and different points of view enrich overall understanding of what are usually complex and rapidly changing circumstances. Acquiring and developing   skills – such as listening, asking questions, reflecting and thinking – were once considered part of basic training. However, experience suggests that this may no longer be the case.

The language in which the narrative develops is also crucial. In order that all participants are able to share a common understanding about the meaning of the events and experiences described, the language must be meaningful. It must reflect common usage to include and widen participation rather than rely on pseudo-scientific 'professional' jargon, which only excludes.

The capacity to tell stories is one of the distinguishing features of human beings. We commonly recall our lives in narrative form and remember significant events as a story to tell. Case studies are often used to illustrate points in a theory or to make clear how something can be applied to real-life situations. The case studies that conclude this chapter (and the book) are about two young people; Richard (not his real name), was a young person who had to live for most of his childhood in a variety of different care environments because of circumstances not of his making. Richard lived his life in a world populated by social workers, foster carers, residential staff, teachers, and other professional workers, including psychologists and psychiatrists. Written from the perspective of his last foster carer, this narrative is an attempt to bridge the gap between the 'professional carer' world and the daily life and experiences of a traumatised and damaged child. Steven (also not his real name) came to live in a therapeutic community at the point when he was about to experience a turbulent period in his life which became a real challenge to his sense of self and the development of his identity. The case study describes the effects of this on the adults and other young people living alongside him at this time.

BELIEVING THE IMPOSSIBLE

> *"There's no use trying," she said, "one can't believe impossible things."*
> *"I dare say you haven't had much practice," said the Queen.*
> *"When I was your age, I always did it for half an hour a day. Why, sometimes I've believed as many as six things before breakfast."*

> (Lewis Carroll, *Beyond the Looking Glass*)

For those who work with damaged and traumatised children or young people, believing impossible things doesn't seem too difficult! If I had a pound for every handover meeting I have ever sat in, listening to a bewildered member of staff recount some unbelievable incident from the night before, I would be a rich man by now. The utter amazement with which a senior architect from the Department of Health looked at the damage caused by a young person to his 'indestructible' bedroom (in one of the most up-to-date and well designed secure-units in the country at the time) is a much treasured memory of mine!

The nature of our work demands curiosity and imagination, but from time to time it defies belief. Working and living with uncertainty, and holding on through tortuous confusion and chaos, are vital to the task of engaging with vulnerable and damaged children or young people. Unless this emotional turmoil is understood – and unless is factored into the design and management-systems of the organisations charged with meeting their care, education, or health needs – the consequences will show in inevitable tensions and conflict.

> *The inherent preferences of organisations are clarity, certainty and perfection. The inherent nature of human relationships involves ambiguity, uncertainty and imperfection. How one honours, balances and integrates the needs of both is the real trick of management.*

> (Pascale and Athos 1981)

In *Attention and Interpretation*, Wilfred Bion (1970) makes a link between a poet's description of the mental condition necessary for writing poetry and the work of an analyst. He quotes John Keats who expresses the ideal conditions for writing poetry as *"when a man is capable of being in uncertainties, mysteries and doubts without any irritable reaching after fact and reason"*.

Unfortunately, such ideas do not sit comfortably within what has become established, professional discourse, and today Keats's description would almost certainly not be recognised as representing the ideal conditions for professional practice! Although the particular focus of this book may be on welfare and education services for children, young people and their families, there are wider cultural and political dimensions to the argument. The way in which the notion of control has become the dominating voice in current political ideologies is allied to the increasing degree of coercion in the interpretation of concepts, such as 'in the best interests of the child'. This has a direct bearing on the workings of our social and welfare services, illustrated by the way in which the practice has become driven and directed by a political agenda that is expressed through the language and intention of central policy.

Perhaps the most obvious example of this process can be seen in the changing role of the Probation Service. Whilst the term 'client', which previously described the people with whom the service was working, may not have been the best, it did at least convey the idea that a service was being offered. The pervasive use of the term 'offender' certainly does not convey any such meaning, and as Gregory and Holloway comment:

> *The fact that this word is used even in contexts in which it makes little sense is a clear indication that its use is more about creating a punitive culture than straight forward communication.*

> (Gregory and Holloway, 2005: 47)

The work of the Probation Service has always been community based and for people who have committed offences either as an alternative to a custodial sentence or on their release from custody. The original aims of the service to 'assist, advise and befriend' are now described as 'to enforce the conditions of their (offenders) court orders and release licences and to take whatever steps in their power to protect the public.' I shall explore this in further detail in subsequent chapters, particularly in the discussion in chapter 5 on the current practice issues that face workers in direct situations with children and young people where the assessment and management of risk has taken centre stage.

Another example of the changing discourse of social welfare and education services is the growing use of the language of consumerism. The use of such concepts as 'best value' has permeated both social work and education, whilst the focus on managerial outcomes has spawned a notion of 'quality' and a burgeoning of quality assurance programmes across all types of services and organisations. In a powerful article, *'Quality Assurance as a Social Defence Against Anxiety,'* Anne-Marie Cummins (2002) describes how originally the concept of quality assurance was linked to production values, i.e. to failure rates and 'fitness for use' in manufacturing industries, 'yet in the space of a couple of decades, quality assurance has gone from being an engineering concept with a link to the shop floor to being a managerial one'.

Cummins explores what she describes as the underlying psychic aims of Quality Assurance programmes. She believes that these are intended to provide comfort and to reassure managers in organisations that all is well and that all procedures and regulations are being followed and adhered to. But, as she goes on to say:

> *The desire to know (in order to evaluate) which is central to the methodology of quality assurance masks a deeper desire not to know things which are uncomfortable, unsettling and most definitely not reassuring.*

(Anne-Marie Cummins, 2002: 100)

There are links here to the role that inspection currently plays across services and agencies, and we shall extend this discussion to consider specific examples of how typical approaches in quality-assurance and inspection regimes fail to get 'beneath the skin' when faced with the struggles of trying to engage and work with very delinquent or damaged people.

TRUTH WITHIN OURSELVES

> *TRUTH is within ourselves; it takes no rise*
> *From outward things, whate'er you may believe.*
> *There is an inmost centre in us all,*
> *Where truth abides in fullness; and around,*
> *Wall upon wall, the gross flesh hems it in,*
> *This perfect, clear perception – which is truth.*
> *A baffling and perverting carnal mesh*
> *Binds it, and makes all error: and, to KNOW,*
> *Rather consists in opening out a way*
> *Whence the imprisoned splendour may escape,*
> *Than in effecting entry for a light*
> *Supposed to be without.*

(Robert Browning, *Paracelsus*)

Browning's poem eloquently and provocatively encapsulates much of the previous argument. Issues of evidence and knowledge loom large in contemporary debates; the question is, however, what do we mean by evidence, and what kind of knowledge are we talking about? The knowledge referred to by Browning suggests something inside each one of us that needs drawing out and nurturing, rather than a knowledge 'shone' into us by external benefactors, who are perhaps well-meaning but not necessarily so.

The purpose of *How Nurture Protects Children* is to explore and challenge much of current thinking and practice in all aspects of work with children and young people. It also aims to stimulate others to share in this questioning at a time when such a venture may be deemed unnecessary and – in the face of daunting workloads, ever growing mountains of paper and electronic data sets – just too arduous. My concern, however, is that it is in the very nature of the work that we do to be critical, to ask questions and admit when we genuinely do not know the answers, and to acknowledge and struggle with what can appear to be an overwhelming tide of bewildering feelings and emotions.

I invite you to take up this challenge and read on, so defying the received wisdom that nowadays no-one is interested in these issues. If I can 'make my own words' as I go, so can you.

Chapter 1

Knowledge, experience and thinking

'O fret not after knowledge – I have none
And yet the Evening listens'
'O thou whose face hath felt the Winter's wind'

John Keats, 1818

A frog asks a centipede, 'How do you manage to make all your legs work so smoothly together? I have four to think about and that's enough.' The centipede starts to think about the question and from that moment on, he can't walk anymore!

There are times when what we have to think about becomes so overwhelming or appears so complex the only thing that we are able to do is to stop thinking about it. The incidents and situations people working directly with traumatised children and young people may hear about or witness sometimes fall into that category – they are just too hard to think about! The devastation this can cause to the personal and family life of frontline workers should not be underestimated. What is clear from experience is that the way in which they are helped to cope and come to terms with these issues is critical, not only for their own ongoing health and well-being but for their ability to continue to provide support to their case load of children and families, or to the pupils in their classroom.

Managers in organisations also have responsibility for ensuring that their management and supervision of staff is consistent and appropriate to the nature of the work undertaken. Much like an onion with its skins upon skins, the wider systems within which organisations and staff teams operate – right up to the level of government – need to have an equally clear understanding of what it feels like to work in environments that involve dealing with the most horrifying of human behaviour and its consequences.

INFORMATION EXPLOSION

Information explosion is a term that describes the rapidly increasing amount of published information and the effects of this abundance of data. As the amount of available data grows, the problem of managing the information becomes more difficult, which can lead to information overload.

(Wikipedia: The Free Encyclopaedia)

Whilst the origin of the term 'information explosion' seems to have its roots in the rapid expansion of the internet, it is a very apt phrase to describe some of the processes that are currently threaded through our human service agencies. The phenomenon of 'information overload' means that particular forms of data too easily become confused with knowledge, so it is assumed that the more data that is available the more we will know!

There is a deeper issue to be considered here and it concerns that part of our humanity that craves for certainty. We have a need to know because we have a need to be in control, and the desire for certainty is never stronger than in those situations where we feel vulnerable or somehow exposed. This is an aspect of the current and fierce raging debate about global warming and the perceived endangerment to the environment. At one level, the issue presents a fundamental challenge to our place in the ecology of the living world: we are presented with the intolerable fact that we seemingly cannot control the processes of evolution! We find living with such doubts and confusions messy and unsettling. We have a basic need for order, for structure, and for unfailing routine.

Counterbalancing this need for certainty and control is another dimension to our human nature: the drive that urges us to discover new things and gives us the capacity to take risks. Mountains have always been climbed, deserts crossed, and jungles explored. Men have even walked on the moon. It is this yearning for discovery and adventure that underpins the history of science and steers scientific experimentation. We are naturally curious about our world and we want to know about its origins, but in addition we want to ask questions about its meaning. Whilst science may be primarily concerned with questions about how order in the natural and physical world emerged from pre-eternal chaos, it also has legitimate interest in questions of value and meaning. As Tom Billington points out, it is only relatively recently that the division between 'arts and science' has become fixed.

> *Contemporary psychology and also sociology originated in the 19th century as part of that maelstrom of human invention that resulted in a division of labour between the arts and sciences, identified specifically as 1867 (Williams, 1983). Hitherto, knowledge relating to the nature of human feelings, thinking and being in the world would have been contemplated across different sites of endeavour. Philosophers and writers, for example, might be considered to possess key knowledge about the human condition, both in respect of our inner and external human worlds. However, the thrust for more organised*

modes of inquiry became unstoppable.

(Billington, T. 2009: 4)

In our current education system, those activities associated with what are designated either 'science' or 'the arts' are disconnected. Their modes of thinking are categorised into rational on the one hand, and creative or imaginative on the other. Throughout its history, however, science has sought its answers not just through specific and supposedly rational methods of enquiry, but by harnessing creativity and imagination.

To take an example from the physical sciences, the late Brian Goodwin, a distinguished and creative biologist, was described in his *Guardian* obituary (09 August 2009) as:

> ... *a key founder of theoretical biology, a branch of mathematical biology that uses the methods of mathematics and physics to understand processes in biology. He became a leading advocate of holistic science, in which emotion and intuition rank equally with rational analysis of natural phenomena, aiming to lead science away from an amoral notion of control to an ethical sense of participation in the unfolding story of life on Earth. Goodwin's dedication to holistic theory and practice led him to advocate that science and the humanities should be merged.*

Within the scientific community there are still ongoing and lively arguments not just about what constitutes valid scientific methodology, but whether or not it is possible to conceptualise a value-base for scientific endeavours. For Brian Goodwin, science was not and never could be a neutral activity. The key question he wrestled with was how it might be possible to reconcile and incorporate into a coherent and single model the 'subjective and intuitive' with the 'objective'.

Whilst he firmly believed that the '*knowledge you get from science is real knowledge about the real world,*' Goodwin was equally clear that there are other and equally valid ways of knowing:

> *I believe that there is a whole scientific methodology that needs to be developed on the basis of what is called the intuitive way of knowing. It's not something that's vaguely subjective and artistic, it's a definite way of knowing the world. In fact, it's absolutely essential to creative science. All the great scientists, Einstein, Feynman, you name them, would say intuition is the way they arrived at their basic insights ... The famous guys are allowed to say this. The rest of us have to pretend*

that we're really basing everything on hard fact, proceeding to gener-
alise as Francis Bacon told us to, not seeing a new whole intuitively.

(Brian Goodwin 1997)

In this reference, Goodwin alludes to another of his ideas that is of interest
to us. This is his concern about the relationship of parts to the whole, and
the importance of applying *'intuitive ways of knowing about wholes as well as
analytical ways of knowing about parts, which takes us into what may be called a
science of qualities'* (ibid.).

We shall consider later the ways in which it is always critical to think about
the 'whole' situation in child-protection scenarios, whilst at the same time re-
maining aware of – and being involved in – the different 'parts' of a developing
narrative. Achieving and maintaining this balance between intuitive and analytical thinking is vital ground for creative and safe practice. This, so Goodwin
argues in his inimitable style, has enormous implications for education at all
levels and is relevant to issues in current professional education and training.

> *In our educational system today, we focus on the analytical, and we just
> leave the intuitive alone. In fact we tend to deny or ignore it. Just as
> we've been kicking shit out of Nature for 400 years, we've been doing
> the same to that part of our nature that we call subjectivity or intuition.*

(ibid.)

Tom Billington, whilst affirming that *'any work with children which is justified
by recourse to the authority of psychology, therefore, must primarily pay homage
to the notion of human relationships'*, does not 'argue simplistically against ob-
jectivity'. His position is rather that:

> *... there is a need to consider the fracture between knowledge and ex-
> perience which lies at the heart of our work. It is not the intention to
> privilege experience over knowledge in this paper, however, but rather
> to suggest the need for a more conscious acknowledgment and sophis-
> ticated understanding of their relationship. A tentative step forward
> would be to establish that in the study and practice of psychology in
> education we take more seriously the importance of the relationships
> we share with children and young people, not only as an ethical proce-
> dure but as part of the social construction of any knowing that accrues.*

(Billington op. cit. 4)

THE QUEST FOR CERTAINTY

In part, at least, the quest for certainty and the desire to control what is terrifying is a result of the anxiety-provoking nature of the tasks in which we engage – and this is especially so in child-protection work. Whilst in subsequent chapters we shall explore the implications of this for teachers, social care staff and foster carers in particular; it is interesting to note how this area of huge concern and wide public interest provides a fulcrum for many of the issues raised previously, including the over reliance on procedures, protocols and data-orientated systems for recording and reporting. In addition, there are clear effects arising from the professionalisation of child-protection work, such as the emergence of a separate and discrete area of practice designed to satisfy the need for control and certainty and perceived to have come from expert knowledge.

As we shall see in chapter 2, it is not lack of information that has been identified as a problem in child protection enquiry reports; it is the lack of co-ordinated thinking about the meaning of the data entered in the numerous information boxes of the standard forms used by different agencies. Human relationships are always multi-dimensional. When we meet another person, irrespective of the context, we use the variety of our senses to fashion a picture of them. We do this in order to help us make necessary judgements about such matters as their honesty and integrity or their feelings towards us. To build up this picture, we may use 'hard' data that we have gathered beforehand about their education, qualifications or previous jobs. Some of the information we use might be 'softer' data acquired through earlier informal contacts with mutual acquaintances or more likely based on our experience of meeting the person. In other words, we use a combination of facts (knowledge) and feelings (experience) to make judgements and come to conclusions.

What seems to have happened with models for evaluation and performance-measurement in social welfare, education, and health care is that in the quest for certainty – and with false assurances about the reliability of 'knowledge' over 'experience' – narrow and closed views about how scientific enquiry proceeds have come to dominate. We have lost the capacity to hold together quantitative (objective) and qualitative (subjective) data collected through the routine activities of daily work, and with it lost the capacity to take the experiences of those involved in those processes seriously.

In order to think about and evaluate situations, measure the outcomes of programmes of work, or plan future interventions; managers and workers are required to process both objective and subjective forms of data and turn the information before them into coherent accounts of human behaviour.

However, we have become obsessed with so-called objective measurements and so rigidly straitjacketed by data collection methods, which rely on coding for statistical analysis that we are in danger of losing the skills required for understanding the complex human situations the data is supposedly recording. These vital skills are the ability to think and reflect, to make connections between apparently disparate events, to trust our reactions to people or situations and use them as a source of clinical information, and to use imagination to stimulate fresh insight. Given the truly awful nature of the material that may have to be confronted in complex and emotionally charged child-protection cases, professional workers are perhaps all too grateful for the official and sanctioned opportunity not to think, but merely to record.

NURTURE GROUPS: USING NARRATIVE FOR EVALUATING EFFECTIVENESS

Collecting and collating information to track children's progress in school has always been a required component of nurture group work. Although the primary purpose of the Boxall Profile (see chapter 4) is to help focus thinking on the particular needs of individual children and to plan for how these might be best addressed, the profile is also a tool for the ongoing monitoring of children's progress both whilst they are in the group and when they have returned full-time to their mainstream class.

There have been two substantial research projects undertaken with the explicit purpose of evaluating the effectiveness of nurture groups (Cooper and Whitebread, 2007; Reynolds et al., 2009). Over the past ten years or so, a number of smaller studies have been produced which also attempted to evaluate the effectiveness of nurture groups. These range from very small studies in single schools to larger projects involving clusters of schools or even whole local authority provision.

Whilst these reports are invariably positive about the impact of nurture groups on children and their teachers and parents, the problem remains that their methodologies, the scale of the studies, and the information collected vary to such an extent that it has not been possible to draw their findings together in such a way as to produce a coherent and credible set of conclusions. In 2007, the Nurture Group Network commissioned independent researchers to identify – from the reports collected over the years – a series of key messages about nurture groups and in particular the contributing factors to their success (Goldman and Cook 2008). Whilst this study was able to show the consistency in the reports regarding many of the features contributing to the success of nurture group interventions, it was not of a scope that could provide a common framework for future evaluation work.

In order to address this issue (at the same time as the above work was commissioned), the Nurture Group Network decided to attempt a much larger project to devise a standardised model for the evaluation of nurture groups in primary schools. The aim of the project was that the evaluation format produced by the Network could, and indeed should, be used by all schools and local authorities across the United Kingdom for the purposes of evaluating the effectiveness of their nurture group provision. Data collected in this standardised format on a national scale would clearly make a strong and compelling argument for nurture groups and would be in sufficient detail to persuade policy makers of their effectiveness. In a time of increasing constraints on resources, the availability of this kind of data becomes even more urgent.

The issue to be resolved was what was meant by effectiveness and what kind of data or information might best be used show this? In recent years, the priorities for central policy-making in education have been about standards, levels of attainment, behaviour and school attendance. Most nurture group studies, including the larger research projects, have tended to focus on these issues in one way or another. Underpinning nurture groups, however, is a set of ideas about children's learning being developmental in nature; the importance of the classroom as a safe base for learning in a school environment; the importance of attachment relationships for overcoming barriers to learning; developing children's use of language; and building up resilience and self-esteem through nurturing experiences. There are also values that are integral to nurture group practice, such as being non-judgmental about children's behaviour; understanding behaviour as communication; and supporting and valuing parents' and carers' relationships with their children.

In developing an evaluation framework, it seemed essential to challenge the conventional ideas about what constitutes effectiveness and the fixed notions of what is meant by evidence. Whilst acknowledging that, for political and resource-attracting reasons, showing a statistical improvement in children's behaviour and attendance is required, the heart of nurture groups and the real 'secret of their success' lies in the matrix of relationships that surround each group and which includes the children, teachers, parents and others who make up a whole school community. Getting this sort of material into an evaluation framework and thus confirming the value and importance of the experiences of all those involved with a nurture group was a greater challenge.

Following a tendering process, a contract was agreed between the Nurture Group Network and the Educational Psychology Department in the University of Manchester for the development of a model to include the identification of the areas and criteria that would be incorporated into the evaluation format, to pilot the format, and to present a final version for approval and implementation.

As part of this contract, a second university department, the Educational Psychology Department in the University of Sheffield, was invited to join the project. The particular contribution sought from this department, through the work of Professor Tom Billington, was to think about how using narrative approaches in developing an evaluative framework could result in capturing the experiences of those directly involved (in terms of what their nurture group meant to them), and how this evaluation could give value to their responses. This was to be achieved through a pilot study initially aimed at engaging with nurture group staff in a manner that made sense to them and valued their expertise, and which would then represent as data something of their experiences – in a manner which would be meaningful to others.

The attraction of using a narrative approach was the perceived ability of the model to make contact with what was actually happening in a nurture group, i.e. in the lives of the individuals involved, in the particular individual and group experiences, and in the wider network of group relationships – the quality of which would ultimately determine the 'success' of any nurture group. The constraints of a pilot study precluded the involvement of other key people in the process (notably parents), but the envisaged final model obviously needed to have the potential to be used for this wider purpose.

The overall requirement for the evaluation project, therefore, was to not only provide a framework for collecting data about children's performance in nurture groups (using a standardised set of instruments); but also to develop a narrative model that would enable children, teachers and parents to think and talk about what goes on in their nurture groups. Whilst this latter material encapsulates the unique experiences of each group, once it is brought together the narratives provide a powerful and compelling account of what the nurture group experience means to those most directly affected.

The feedback from the narrative pilot has been largely positive. The final framework will be published shortly, and will hopefully convey the experience of the early pilots. In their initial responses, teachers and support staff indicated that they found the narrative approach to be affirming of their work, because it echoed the ways in which they were already engaging with the children in their nurture groups – i.e. with respect and a sense of human connection. In addition, it offered them a space for reflection that they did not normally experience.

This example from the Nurture Group Network illustrates the importance to evaluation studies of engaging with the people involved in a project or venture, particularly where the object of the study is their actual, lived experience. In this case, whilst it is clearly of relevance to know to what extent children's behaviour, attendance at school, or attainment levels might improve following time in a nurture group, the core of the nurture group experience is about how barriers to leaning are overcome. This is through both recognising the difficulties the children have in making or sustaining relationships, and in the provision of a set of thoughtful, relational experiences with other children and empathic adults.

To ignore the experience of children and adults directly involved with a nurture group or who are part of the wider school community is not only fundamentally disrespectful but misses hugely important opportunities to learn more about what makes the groups work. In this case, using narrative allowed voices that would not normally have been heard to make a significant contribution to the design of the evaluation framework. Billington points out that whilst the use of qualitative research methodologies has increased in recent years as they have become more acceptable as ways to provide evidence about 'complex social situations', the use of narrative '*has arisen out of the more widespread popularity of autobiography which in psychology and education has taken the form of "insider" or "user" accounts ... These new insider accounts perform an important function for they bring into question the accuracy or relevance of our professionalised representations.*' (Billington op. cit. 5) We shall see the relevance and application of this later on in relation to more complex practice situations and settings.

EDUCATION AND TRAINING

Changes and developments in the education and training of professionals in all aspects of social care, education, and other related disciplines involved with children, young people, and their families might well be topics for a complete book. My purpose here is to pull together some of the connections between policy, practice and training to show how in recent years the course of central policy and its ensuing emphases on monitoring and auditing has resulted in the emergence of a practice culture dominated by protocols and procedures, and which is target driven and bureaucratic. All of this, together with other pressures that have been brought to bear on the higher education sector, have had a direct effect on the content and teaching processes of initial and post-qualifying training programmes.

Tony Jeffs and Jean Spence (2007/08) write about the education and training of youth workers specifically, but many of their points are highly relevant to issues in higher education as a whole. Their criticisms about the quality of training echo those that that have been levelled against training programmes designed for other disciplines, e.g., social work and teaching. They offer a serious critique of many of the recent trends in higher education and in particular on the quality of much present-day teaching and learning. From the starting point of the *'Further and Higher Education Act'* (1992), they summarise:

> *The accumulated impact has been to reconfigure the balance between management, administration, teaching and research. Marketisation has injected competition into each and every corner of the sector, strengthening the autonomy of management, bureaucratising systems and subjecting academic issues to pressures external to issues of educational worth and intellectual validity.*

(Jeffs and Spence 2007/08: 138)

The shift in the responsibility for funding individual involvement in higher education from state to student has re-focused the priorities of individuals on outcomes and qualifications, and the priorities of institutions on student numbers and financial viability. This latter concern (to increase student numbers) has led inevitably to questions about the academic standard of people entering professional qualifying courses and the nature of the training they receive. (Social Work Task Force, Interim Report, July 2009).

Jeffs and Spence make reference to the increasing modularisation of many courses and the subsequent breaking down of boundaries between professional disciplines. Interestingly, they draw our attention to a series of unintended consequences that they perceive have followed these developments whilst acknowledging the current preference for both features. The advantages of modularisation are often cited as giving students greater flexibility to determine their overall course content and as providing opportunities to mix with students from other disciplines who are also interested in a particular module topic. However, in moving from module to module, students rarely have the opportunity to build relationships with other students or with their teachers:

> *Students bounce from module to module, sitting alongside others they scarcely know and seldom meet again. William Morris noted that the division of labour led to the 'division of men,' likewise modularisation divides and isolates students and staff.*

(Jeffs and Spence 2007/2008: 142)

Achieving the integration of training programmes for workers of all disciplines is one of the main purposes of the Children's Workforce Development Council (CWDC) established in 2005. Tasked with creating a common framework of qualifications and training pathways, the CWDC has responsibilities for workers across social care and early years. Their remit does not include teachers or learning support staff, but it does include educational psychologists. Whilst there are many advantages in identifying the core skills required for work with children and families – irrespective of the particular discipline for which an individual student may be seeking qualification – the CWDC appears reluctant to suggest any intellectual model to inform this training or any theory-base upon which the development of skills may be built.

Jeffs and Spence also question the extent to which, by integrating courses and teaching in modules, students are enabled to imbibe and absorb the particular history and distinctive values of their chosen area whilst also having the opportunity to study the roots from which other related disciplines have developed. Acquiring this historical perspective would allow students the freedom to contextualise and to question the stated values and aims of their discipline.

> *Just as modularisation fragments the student experience so it fragments knowledge ... Aims, objectives and outcomes written in formulaic ways allow students to predict what is required of them, and for the unit to be picked-up and discarded by any lecturer – then picked up again and discarded by their successors.*

(ibid. 143)

This is part of a much wider argument that goes to the core of what higher education has become, and it charts the change in teaching direction and the processes of learning in the sector as a whole.

> *Outcomes driven processes curtail and in the case of pre-packaged programmes seek to remove the opportunities for teachers to give expression to what Palmer refers to as the 'capacity for connectedness' to 'join self and subject' (1998:11) thereby linking ideas and enabling student and teacher alike to move beyond the merely relevant 'what is' towards a liberatory sense of 'what might be.*

(ibid. 144)

AN IDEAS BOX?

Many of the themes touched on above recur throughout the book where their further exploration is in relation to critical aspects of practice. In some respects, it may be useful to regard this chapter as the 'ideas box' for Making My Own Words and use it as a reference point for the later discussions. Whilst such issues as what constitutes reliable 'evidence' when assessing risk, the importance of narrative for understanding complex family-child protection situations, and the crucial role of attachment relationships and nurture are key themes, the wider issues raised in the previous section on education and training are also central to this book's main argument.

The design and delivery of courses in higher education and especially in those areas of study associated with professional qualification have moved towards what Jeffs and Spence describe as 'pre-packaged programmes', modular in format, prescriptive in content, and offering little space for students to explore beyond the narrow confines of the curriculum. An allied factor of concern is the emphasis on providing students with skills and competencies for practice with considerably less attention being given to the teaching of theory or encouraging the development of thinking and reflection.

There have always been concerns raised about the adequacy of qualifying training in preparing students for the realities of the workplace. I can well remember newly qualified workers being on the receiving end of disparaging remarks along the lines of: 'What did they teach you in college!' However, there was in the past at least recognition that it was the task of a newly qualified practitioner, whether in a social work team or a school class room, to apply the theory they had been taught in college or university in practice. And it was the purpose of supervision or the 'probationary year' to bring theory and practice together so the practitioner could understand them in the light of hard experience. The current lack – and so it seems actual disregard – of theory has implications for practice:

> The gradual displacement of theory by skills is removing from practitioners the ability to make their own theory, to engage in critical investigative conversations and construct alternatives to the status quo … Familiarity with theory makes professional choices possible and under-pins the capacity for reflective practice.

(ibid.159)

In both social care and education, there are high expectations that newly qualified workers entering the work place will be able to take on their allocated workload, perform competently, and manage the bureaucracy. The fact remains, however, that despite the levels of denial, working with troubled and distressed children and families is intense and makes heavy demands on practitioners, irrespective of their qualification or discipline. As we shall see, when confronted by people who may be extremely damaged, highly manipulative, or both, a lack of thinking and the inability to reflect on situations and events have, on occasion, lead to real human tragedy. This issue is not just a matter of individual judgement; the wider systems and the organisations responsible for services also need to be able to think. This capacity and function of organisations is an essential part of providing the support and containment needed by practitioners.

There are some signs that there is a growing awareness of these problems in the way workers are being prepared for their professional roles and duties. In the case of social work, for example, the government established the Social Work Task Force (SWTF) in 2008 to conduct a 'nuts and bolts' review of the profession and to advise on the shape and content of a 'comprehensive reform programme for social work'. The wider context within which the task force was set up included continuing concerns about the state of social-service departments and the apparent failure of these departments to respond to the recommendations of Lord Laming following the death of Victoria Climbié and the subsequent tragedy of baby Peter Connelly. Lord Laming's second report, *'The Protection of Children in England: A Progress Report'* (12 March 2009), gave extra impetus to the work of the SWTF, and an interim report was published in June 2009. This report highlighted a number of areas for further consultation, but already the task force members were recognising serious problems related to recruitment and retention, training, supervision and management, and burdensome workloads made worse by inadequate IT systems and too much bureaucracy!

The final report of the SWTF was published in November 2009, and it confirmed many of the findings from their earlier report, including the need for manageable workloads and proper IT systems for the administration of case loads; high-quality supervision and training; a review of pay and conditions of service to aid recruitment and retention; an overhaul of the training for new entrants to the profession, aimed at improving the quality of graduates and newly qualified social workers; and a compulsory probationary year to be served. In addition, an independent National College of Social Work is to be established to represent and strengthen the voice of all social workers.

The government has committed to implementing all fifteen of the task force's recommendations and time will tell what impact this will make.

Achieving the kind of changes outlined in the SWTF report will not just be a matter of government decree. As we have seen, and as I will illustrate in the coming chapters, it is cultural change at the deepest and highest levels that is required, which means a shift in the mindsets of policy makers, managers and practitioners. It is how this may be brought about to which we now turn.

Chapter 2

Mind the gap

Between the experience of living a normal life at this moment on the planet and the public narratives being offered to give a sense to that life, the empty space, the gap, is enormous.

John Berger

One of the strands running through the enquiry reports that have routinely followed some crisis or appalling incident in social care is the fact that the 'victim' and their family had previously been well known to a whole range of workers and services. About the specific and terrible circumstances that surrounded the death of Victoria Climbié, Lord Laming commented:

> *Victoria was not hidden away. It is deeply disturbing that during the days and months following her initial contact with Ealing Housing Department's Homeless Persons' Unit, Victoria was known to no less than two further housing authorities, four social services departments, two child protection teams of the Metropolitan Police Service (MPS), a specialist centre managed by the NSPCC, and she was admitted to two different hospitals because of suspected deliberate harm. The dreadful reality was that these services knew little or nothing more about Victoria at the end of the process than they did when she was first referred to Ealing Social Services by the Homeless Persons' Unit in April 1999.*

(Laming 2003)

A similar catalogue of statutory services' involvement also featured in the more recent tragic death of the baby, Peter Connelly. As part of their coverage of the story, a number of newspapers published timelines, reporting the numerous visits by professional workers to the family's home, a series of child-protection and case meetings, and the attendance by mother and child to various medical appointments. The reports included a further list of scheduled appointments that the family had failed to attend, along with details of other significant events in Peter's short life.

As summed up by the newspaper, *The Independent*:

> *A baby who was beaten, bruised and left to die by his guardians was seen 60 times by social workers but was never taken into care. The child was seen 18 times by council staff, 37 times by health workers and five times by welfare officers, yet no one rescued him from his abusers before he died.*

(*The Independent*, 12 November 2008)

The point made by Lord Laming is that it not just enough to know about something or someone. It is how that information is used and what sense is made of it that matters. The Department for Children Schools and Families' research report on serious case reviews, *'Analysing child deaths and serious injury through abuse and neglect'* comments;

> *It is what is done with information, rather than its simple accumulation, that leads to more analytic assessments and safer practice.*

(DCSF Report RR023 2008: 2)

The above statements also serve to illustrate the difference that exists between knowing about someone and knowing someone in the truly personal sense that signifies the existence of a relationship.

The pertinent and immediate questions that surfaced from the cases studied in the review included why – with all this information available – the professional workers involved could seemingly make no coherent sense of the underlying realities of the events and circumstances in the day-to-day life of these children and their families? And what are some of the factors that contributed to this state of affairs?

In Lord Laming's original report on Victoria Climbié, he is scathingly critical of the professional competence of a number of workers and dismissive of what he considers an over reliance on the excuse of 'too much bureaucracy' as the reason for their lack of good practice. In fact, he comments, 'the extent of the failure to protect Victoria was lamentable. Tragically, it required nothing more than basic good practice being put into operation. This never happened.'

However, and this is another theme to which we shall be returning, fixing blame on individuals is another toxic feature of the current culture for professional workers. Whilst there should be a proportional place for individual accountability in any analysis of an event as serious as the death of a child, there are also wider and broader systemic issues to be addressed. These are invariably complex and deep-seated, requiring more deliberation than can be encompassed by simple arguments about 'too much paper work'.

DATA DUMPING

There are several layers to unwrap in trying to understand the reasons why professional workers, who have access to large amounts of information about the circumstances of individual children and their families, are not able to process this information in ways that inform and modify their practice. Some of this is a result of the way in which information is gathered and the perceptions that workers have as to why it is collected. The over-prioritising of statistical returns for the purposes of auditing extends across all public services. It becomes a driver for amassing information that, once consigned to an excel spreadsheet and passed upwards and onwards, is lost to practitioners for the purposes of collation and analysis. This analysis is essential for making sense of the human experiences that the statistics are intended to capture. This is the phenomenon I have described as 'data dumping', when between the act of gathering information and implementing further action, no space is allowed for reflective thinking about actual experiences.

In an important and challenging research article, Karen Broadhurst and her colleagues argue that *'current attempts to increase safety through formalisation of organisational procedures and their enactment by IT systems, may have had a contrary effect.'* Furthermore:

> *The study was focused on the impact of performance management on organisational decision making and specifically on attributions of blame. During our fieldwork, we observed that workers at the front-door faced acute challenges to safe practice. Imperatives to safeguard children and support families appeared at odds with, rather than enhanced by, new modes of e-governance and associated performance targets. In particular, the immutable timescales set for the completion of the initial assessment inevitably pushed workers to make quick categorisations based on, at best, one home visit. Equally, the standardised and complex assessment forms appeared to engender a range of problematic recording practices.*

> (Broadhurst et al. 2009: 2)

The aim of her article is to demonstrate from field work examples how the pressure on managers and social workers to process referrals and undertake and record initial assessments within prescribed time scales creates what she calls *'latent error conditions'*. Contributing to these conditions are the 'short cuts' that managers and workers routinely take in the course of their work in order to achieve the specified targets, the consequences of which may be that in the case of individual families poor safeguarding decisions are made. The design of the IT systems for recording initial referrals and assessments exacerbates the potential for error. Broadhurst found that *'data input demands seriously eroded valuable face-to-face time with children and their parents/carers.'*

> *In social services, priority needs to be given to reduce the distance between workers, family and community that many studies have cited (by both service users and front line workers) as central to good practice (Pithouse and Holland, 1999; Gray, 2002; Ruch, 2005). We have seen that the IT-enabled, performance-driven IAS has created further distance between worker and service user, offering instead a scientistic veneer of codes, risk scores and metrics.*

(ibid. 15)

Information gathered by individual services and agencies is rarely brought together in a context whereby its meaning may be thought about and interpreted or used to develop a continuing narrative account of evolving events. Although tools such as the Common Assessment Framework are intended for the collation of different views and therefore intended to address these issues, the context and processes by which the assessment is completed does not and cannot address questions as to how meaning may be ascribed to the data that has been collected.

These are the kind of 'gaps' that concern us, a number of which are highlighted in Karen Broadhurst's research. The increasing distance between professional workers and the daily lives of the people in need of their help and support is a result of demands – made on managers and workers alike – to achieve targets and to ensure information is recorded in ways that facilitate the purposes of audits rather than reflecting the processes of the work itself. There is also a gap in discourse, exemplified in the different ways of speaking about the world in professional jargon and the regular intercourse of daily life.

WHAT DO WE MEAN BY PROFESSIONAL?

There is a vast literature on the topic of what is meant by the term 'professional' and the impact that the growth of so-called 'professionalisation' has had on various aspects of human services.

Rutty (1998), writing about the professionalisation of nursing, states that in order for an area of activity to be legitimately called a profession, it must have a sound and unique knowledge or theory base. He links this to concepts of autonomy and the establishing of a professional organisation, which requires some form of registration for the validation of practice. In addition, something about specific and accredited educational routes to 'qualification' could be added, as well as regulatory frameworks that enshrine a set of values and guidelines for high standards of practice and conduct.

David Kalisch (1990), in an interesting and provocative article points out,

> *The [usual] arguments in favour of social controls like professionalisation always stress the interest of the client/consumer, the safeguards against fraud, quackery, charlatanism, well-meaning incompetence and the like, the greater range of service to clients/consumers, and the wider audience [market] that respectability and control will bring.*

(Kalisch 1990)

This is a slightly tongue-in-cheek portrayal of the positive effects of professionalisation, as his main argument is much more caustic and critical of the exploitative and controlling impact that he ascribes to this process:

> *Dependencies are created, empires built and nests lavishly lined. Restrictive practices, closed shops, protection and collusion follow in their wake and are their mode of operation.*

(ibid.)

Dave Andrews (2001) writes about the effects of the process of professionalisation on community work in Australia. Community work is an intriguing area of activity in that its locus is directly concerned with the daily lives and conditions of ordinary people in the communities where they live and work. He describes professionalisation as it has emerged for those involved in community work;

> *To begin with people who wanted to be involved in community work just got involved in community work. Then various parties involved in community work pressed for there to be more adequate training.*
> *Then those with more adequate training pressed for a professional association. Then those in the professional association pressed for the support of the system to impose certification requirements on the practice of community work. So now there is the situation where voluntary community work goes largely unrecognised, unless it is under*

the auspices of professional community work.

(Andrews 2001: 18)

Andrews goes on to explore what he regards as the damaging and negative effects of this process on the ethos and values of community work. The eroding effect is when the responsibility for work previously undertaken in the community by a largely volunteer workforce of local people is moved to an elite cadre of 'professionals' who – by the processes of professionalisation – effectively seal their work off from the influence of local people. Andrews refers to the work of Donald Kraybill et al. (1982) who published a *'controversial list detailing the dangerous effects of professionalisation.'* For our purposes – and to understand more about what we have called the 'gap' between professional discourse and the realities of daily life for most people – three items on Kraybill's list are especially interesting; these are what he calls *'fragmenting reality'*, *'separating people'* and *'making mystery'*.

'Fragmenting reality' refers to the tendency of professionals to specialise and in so doing to lose their focus on the bigger picture and the wider scope of their work. In social-work practice, the tendency towards increased specialism has become a feature of the way services for children and families have evolved. Child protection workers may receive recognition and kudos for having acquired additional, specific expertise; but their 'knowledge' and in turn their practice all too easily become divorced from the wider body of developing knowledge and practice in child-care social work. This places serious limitations on opportunities for the continuing professional development of child-protection workers, but perhaps more critically for practice is that when dealing with specific situations, there may well be communication problems between specialists and generic workers from another (or even the same) agency.

'Separating people' extends the idea of specialism by considering its effect on the way in which professionals within the same area of work tend not to relate to each other as closely as they should or need to. There is also a tendency for the specialist, in developing their specific expertise, to become distanced from the lives of the people to whom they are supposed to be offering a service.

It is an interesting paradox that at a time when there is such a concentrated focus on 'joint working', 'integrated services' and 'multi-agency' approaches, the desire for a more holistic organisation of services is counter-balanced by opposing forces for increased specialism and by an inflated valuation of expert knowledge.

'*Making mystery*' alludes to what we have referred to as the discrete discourse that professionals use to describe their activity, and which is administratively reflected in the formats devised for the purposes of recording information.

Specialised language and verbalised procedures are intended to create a mysterious shroud over professional practice. (Kraybill et al. op cit: 228)

In part, these formats serve to reinforce the illusion of expertise and provide government with the sought for re-assurance that all is well with the world. This comforting note of reassurance is also struck by the processes of current inspection regimes. It is worthy of note that in the months leading up to the exposure of the terrible and terrifying conditions in which Peter Connelly lived his short life, the local authority charged with the responsibility for his safety and protection received a good inspection report from the inspecting authority, Ofsted. More recent disputes about the reliability of this report have called current inspection practice and the inspectorates' relationship with government even further into question.

THE EXAMPLE OF FOSTER CARE

Foster care provides fertile ground for exploring a number of the points made above in more detail. Foster carers are required to provide accommodation and care for some of the most vulnerable and challenging children and young people in the looked-after population, or for those involved with youth justice services, e.g., young people on remand or placed as an alternative to custody.

The essence of foster care is the provision of care for children and young people in circumstances that replicate – as closely as possible – normal family life, and also to provide them with a stable domestic environment. Foster carers have traditionally been recruited from a wide range of social and ethnic groups, the priorities of the recruitment criteria being the availability of suitable accommodation and a demonstrable set of skills and personal qualities. Prospective carers are formally assessed by a social worker, and their registration is confirmed by the decision and recommendation of a Fostering Panel. Although financial remuneration has always been part of their terms and conditions, being a foster carer has not generally been regarded as an opportunity for earning an income or pursuing a career path.

In recent years, foster care has become the preferred option for providing care to the majority of looked-after children unable to live at home. The reasons for this are beyond the present scope of our discussion, but the decline in the number of children's residential homes has been a major contributory factor. This decline is in itself a fascinating subject and is relevant in that the reduction is partly a result of the creeping effects of the industrialisation of the terms and conditions for residential staff, such as the introduction of shift work. This is just one element in what has been for this particular social-care workforce a long, drawn-out process of seeking professional parity with their field social-work colleagues. Other factors that played a part in the reduction of residential care for children include a prevalence of high-profile scandals, where children and young people were abused in residential homes and schools, as well as the dramatically increasing costs of providing high-quality residential accommodation with adequate levels of staffing.

Overall, the ability of local authorities and agencies to recruit foster carers at a sufficient rate has not kept pace with the ever-growing demand for placements. This has put increasing pressure on the efforts of local authorities to secure sufficient accommodation for the number of children requiring foster placements. The emergence and initially rapid growth in the number of companies setting themselves up as independent providers of foster care has presented a severe challenge to local authorities.

In the early days of the independent fostering sector, there were large numbers of carers transferring from local authorities to independent providers, and the costs of foster care rose significantly. Although both of these problems have abated, the retention of carers, and the costs of placements have continued to exercise local-authority managers. In general, foster carers have experienced the independent sector as not only providing higher levels of remuneration, which on the whole they feel are justified and necessary in terms of the difficulty and demands of the work, but more importantly the independent sector offers a better and more responsive support network.

The extent to which the emergence of the independent sector has added to the national pool of foster carers is debatable. Official statistics currently estimate that there is a shortfall of around 8,000 in the required number of carers, a deficit which explains at least in part why increased attention is being paid to the issue of their terms and conditions.

As a result of the changing patterns in foster care provision, in which issues of placement costs and remuneration of carers have assumed growing significance, other important questions are also being asked about the nature of the work and the qualities and skills that foster carers require. These questions bring the professionalisation of fostering and the relative merits and demerits of this into sharp focus. At first sight, the activities at the heart of fostering, i.e. providing family experiences for children and young people, do not fit easily with what might be deemed professional work. The reasons and motivation of people who offer themselves as foster carers are not entirely the same as those of people seeking conventional employment. Indeed, when social workers are assessing people's suitability as potential foster carers, they pay careful attention to their motivation and directly address questions such as, 'Are they in it for the money?'

> We recognise that the term "professional" has connotations that do not always seem to fit easily with the foster carers' role. Foster carers take up fostering for a range of reasons that are not necessarily to do with wishing to be a "professional", and which initially appear to be in direct contradiction to the requirements of a "professional". We know that for some people there is a tension in foster care between love and money, and that there is a fear that by more emphasis being put on money, less will be placed on caring and people will be attracted to fostering for financial rewards.

> (The Fostering Network 2008)

The Fostering Network recognises the increasing complexity of this issue and argues that in order to provide the best care to children, many of whom have experienced abusive relationships with adults and who display a range of disturbed behaviours, foster carers need a high level of support and training in order to provide a safe and secure environment for the children – as well as for themselves and their own families. In addition, the Fostering Network argues that foster carers should be granted higher status within the wider workforce and accorded the same respect as members of the other professional networks involved in the delivery of care, education and treatment programmes.

The 2008 paper outlines the increasing range of work required of foster carers and what they contribute to the work of the multi-disciplinary teams, including the central and core business of providing the direct, personal care and the support of substitute parents.

> Foster carers are at the centre of a multi-disciplinary team of professionals who work on behalf of children and young people in public care. They are required to deliver highly personalised care within a professional framework and need to approach what they do in a professional manner: report writing, assessments, home reviews, dealing with paperwork, attending placement agreement meetings, involvement with the police, attending court and giving evidence, managing contact, and doing life-story work. All the while they continue with parenting and meeting the emotional and physical needs of the child

in their care in a way that safeguards the child and themselves.

(The Fostering Network 2008)

Foster carers frequently become part of the bridge for the gaps that exist between the different worlds inhabited by professional workers, children, young people and often their families as well. Foster carers are expected to perform tasks such as 'recording' or 'report writing', using formats alien to the experience of routine family life. At the same time, they are expected to provide an immediate response to any crisis that might blow up, whilst also continuing to offer ongoing family support.

There is another dimension to this dynamic which concerns the experience of foster carers as they begin to take their place in the professional network. Over a good many years now, I have met with foster carers in a variety of settings and contexts: new carers, just through panel, who are anxious but excited; more experienced carers in training and support groups; and worn-out carers, looking for new enthusiasm and energy. In both the latter circumstances, the recurring and repeated complaints are not only about how their role is perceived by professional workers, but about how they are actually treated in their dealings with them. The same is not true of their experience, on the whole, with their agency support workers, although problems can arise in this area as well; but it is almost universally their view of social workers.

The Fostering Network campaign *'together for change'* (2009) is aimed at raising the status of foster carers and achieving greater recognition of their role as integral members of the professional network for looked-after children in foster care. In a survey of foster carers as part of this campaign, it was reported that 96% of the carers surveyed agreed that receiving social-worker support as a carer was important. Of the carers, 75% stated that the support they received from their support social worker was 'excellent', and 96% stated that a good working relationship with a child's social worker was also very important; but only 40% said that the relationship they had experienced was 'good'.

'We are bottom of the heap' has been said to me more than once, along with 'we are always the first to get the blame.' It is undoubtedly true that the vulnerability foster carers feel is related to their emotional proximity to the children and young people in their care. It is also, however, a result of the external culture of fear and blaming that sets the context within which such matters as allegations and complaints are considered and investigated.

A SHORT CASE STUDY

Alison and Robert had been with their carers, Mary and Geoff, for over two years. Both children had suffered serious sexual abuse whilst with their birth family, and the first eighteen months of their foster placement had been very difficult for everyone, with frequent episodes of challengingly defiant behaviour from the children. During this time, Robert had made a number of allegations about Mary and Geoff and whilst none proved to have had any substance, the content of the allegations was thought to mirror the children's experiences of abuse in the past. For Robert, in particular, it was clearly very difficult to differentiate between what had happened previously and what was going on in the present.

Such confusion of experience and mixing up of time is not uncommon with children who have been abused, and we shall consider this phenomenon further in chapter 5. However, in this instance, after two years it was determined by the local authority – without consultation with the foster carers – that Robert should be seen by a therapist and offered individual sessions. Part of the process was meant to involve the carers talking with the therapist after each session and being kept up to speed with any developments. Robert was reluctant to go to therapy, and during the course of the first six sessions he told his therapist that he was being badly treated in the foster home, was made to eat his meals alone and away from the family, and was sent to bed at seven o'clock each evening. The therapist – despite the terms of the counselling arrangements – made no contact with Mary or Geoff. Rather than seek to clarify what Robert was telling her, either with the foster carers or with the fostering agency for which they worked, she made direct contact with the local authority. She recommended that the placement should be terminated immediately and that Robert be placed for a period of respite care in a residential unit whilst an assessment for long-term placement in a therapeutic unit was undertaken. The foster carers were not invited to any of the subsequent case meetings, and so in effect they were excluded from the process of clarification, although they held the most important and relevant material for understanding what might be going on. Fortunately, the information available from visits by both the social worker and the worker from the independent fostering agency, including unannounced visits, together with reports from Annual Reviews and the children's school, meant the situation could be resolved without disruption to the placement or further distress to the children.

RELATIONSHIPS MATTER

In the light of such experiences, it is not difficult to see why foster carers feel they are at the 'bottom of the heap.' Ironically, the relationship that a foster carer has, or is trying to develop, with individual children and young people is often the most valued factor in the lives of those children – and the most promising ground for their healthy growth and personal development. There is much current interest and investment in models of 'specialist fostering', invariably supervised by high-status professionals and often reliant on behavioural approaches. These techniques have to be taught to carers and implemented rigorously with children and young people as part of a wider programme. The effectiveness of the programmes, which are always monitored and evaluated, is usually dependent on the degree to which carers can consistently perform their tasks, and this all takes place in the context of a family environment! I well remember the surprise a consultant psychiatrist expressed at the suggestion that maybe the core tasks of fostering – i.e. caring and supporting children in a context of reliable and consistent family routines whilst a relationship of trust and mutual affection is allowed to develop – might have as much, or even more, therapeutic value than that derived from the targets and star charts of the programme!

The danger in all this is that with growing demands for 'professionalism', which are often reinforced by the recommendations of various 'enquiries' and allied to ideas of specialism and a unique body of knowledge accessible only to professionals, foster carers will be driven even more to seek the false comforts of organisation, accreditation, and the associated trappings of professional recognition.

It is part of the argument of this book that what is required is a reversal of these processes, so that in the context of fostering, for example, the relational role of foster carers becomes acknowledged as the primary intervention – with the role of the professional networks being to find ways to encapsulate that experience, make sense of it, and support its development.

PROFESSIONAL ALIENATION

One of the main criticisms of professionalism is that the acquisition of professional status, whether for social or community workers, inevitably leads to a separation of the new professional community from the very groups in society who were its intended focus for help. The argument is that increased power and self-interest, gained through becoming professional, inevitably lead to a drift away from original and primary aims for social reform or radical social action. In our present environment, the idea of social workers as advocates for social justice gains short shrift amongst those who direct policy and invariably hold the purse strings. Dave Andrews quotes Kay Laursen (1975) from her survey of Australian social work:

It is my contention that professionalism is primarily characterised by self-interest, expressed in a quest for power, economic, social, personal, and political; that professionalism by its very nature makes little difference to the underlying causes of client's problems (it does not, nor does it intend to, change the social structure in any radical way such that the more fundamental causes of problems are dealt with); that when it comes to the crunch, to a choice between "the powers that be" and the welfare of their clients, professionals opt for the former, while simultaneously trying to convince their erstwhile clients that this betrayal is in their best interests; and finally, that professionalism militates against a genuine service to clients because it alienates professionals from their own humanity, and naturally from the common humanity they could share with their client.

(Laursen 1975 in Andrews 2001: 23)

This argument seeks to explain why in probation, social work, community work and youth work, the drive for professional status has produced over time a shift in the centre of the work. It can also be linked to another identifiable, broader change in the nature of welfare services, i.e. a re-balancing of the welfare/control paradigm. The treatment of its young and most vulnerable citizens is a genuine test of any society's core values. Even more so is that society's treatment of young people who are deemed to be delinquent, anti-social or disordered. A cursory study of the changing legal framework over the past 40 years indicates that we are now living in a less tolerant society and that the redefined purposes of the main welfare and education agencies includes much greater emphasis on monitoring, investigation and public protection rather than on supporting or advocating for individuals, families and communities. This is paralleled by the way in which organisations are called to account for their activity through regimes of auditing and inspection, with the emphases of their ever growing bureaucracies being data collection and output measurement.

However, as the above trends move towards increasing professionalism, reliance on 'expertise', more directive statements of purpose, and perhaps what might be described as a more authoritarian approach towards the provision of welfare; there have been counter forces from other directions. Amongst these are an increasing public scepticism about the reliability of so-called professionals and a steady decline in the authority of public institutions and traditional authority figures. Perhaps, as John Berger notes, there is another gap emerging between the belief systems of those who create the policy framework for our public institutions and the perceptions of the wider public about their value and authority.

The gap between increasing authoritarianism in public life and the decreasing levels of respect for authority in wider society is constantly reinforced by media reporting. Writing about social work, Peter Wilby comments:

> No professional group gets such a consistently bad press. Even politicians and estate agents get a more respectful hearing. The press berates failings by doctors, teachers and police, but they often get positive coverage, while social workers get virtually none.

(Peter Wilby, *The Guardian* 17 November 2008)

Overall, this is a very balanced article that explores some of the underlying reasons for the 'bad press' received by social workers, including the deep ambivalence felt within society about their role; and the feeling that the nature of their work is essentially un-newsworthy. Peter Wilby continues, 'most social work is slow and complex. There is no climax, only, perhaps, a painfully engineered improvement in a family's circumstances or a reluctant acceptance that a child has no future at home.'

QUALITY ASSURANCE – A DEFENCE AGAINST ANXIETY

Demonstrating 'quality' has become something of a mantra for public service organisations, and has also become an integral part of the regulatory framework that governs and shapes practice. But, what do the measures that are most frequently used in the spheres of welfare and education really tell us about an organisation and its work? In addition, what actual function do they perform?

The nature of much of the daily work of social workers and other 'front line' practitioners produces high levels of anxiety. This is experienced by the workers themselves as well as by their managers, and it sends shudders through the various systems within which they operate. Risks have to be calculated and decisions have to be made that affect not only the people immediately involved, but their wider family, their social networks, and potentially the general public as well. How this anxiety – and the impact it has on decision making – is managed must become an integral part of the way services operate and taken into account when trying to evaluate their 'effectiveness'. Unconscious processes that influence how decisions are made, and the effects of the sheer 'emotionality' of this work on practitioners, have to be taken seriously. They are essential considerations for safe and effective management, and we shall think more specifically about the implications of this at both managerial and systems levels in later chapters.

Wilby, as noted earlier from his article, seems to have understood something of the complex nature of the social-work task, but there is more to it than that. The work, particularly in high profile areas such as child protection, is not only complex but also messy and difficult, and it provokes a bewildering array of conflicting feelings that generate strong and competing arguments about what may be the right decisions and actions to be taken. This is material which, at a human level, is at best uncomfortable and at worst completely unbearable. Defending against 'too much reality' as T. S. Eliot put it is part of the human condition. In the circumstances of having to deal with something as awful as the abuse or death of a child, the processes of defending against trauma become as active and as potent for the social worker as for the perpetrator.

It is a powerful and compelling argument that, underlying the current preoccupation for gathering information (which is then put towards the ultimate goal of seeking to demonstrate effectiveness and quality), is the desire to make rational and reasonable the sort of experience that – by its very nature – is almost unbelievable and irrational.

SECURE ACCOMMODATION

Locking up children and young people is always a highly controversial subject and is one that arouses extremes of reaction and responses. In many respects, the topics of secure accommodation and restriction of liberty – especially of the young – bring a sharp light onto wider discussions about both the role of welfare services and whether any sense of balance has been achieved within the welfare-control paradigm. Secure units also focus the ambivalence that we feel as a society towards people whose behaviour appals us but for whose circumstances we feel somewhat responsible; we find such things incredibly hard to think about and would rather not know about them, although we retain a somewhat prurient interest in what might be going on behind the high walls.

Whilst most young people confined within what is now designated the secure estate are detained for their offending behaviour, a small proportion are, for welfare reasons, in the care of the part of the estate provided by local authority Secure Children's Homes. Irrespective of the reasons for their detention, what this means in practice is that this population of children and young people are amongst the most delinquent and damaged in society. Although they may have been convicted of the most serious and grave crimes in some instances, the overwhelming evidence about the majority of these young people indicates that they are amongst the most disadvantaged and deprived of their age group, and many have experienced serious abuse. It is a salutary and depressing picture:

Secure units are dealing with young people who are likely to have had disrupted and disturbed experiences of family life from a very early age and many have been subject to various and often multiple forms of abuse by adults from whom they might have expected better. For a large number of these young people this has resulted in episodes of being in care, running away and fractured links with any form of stable home life. A significant number of the young people have had difficulties at school with both teachers and other children. This has resulted later on in either exclusion or truancy with the associated problems of having large amounts of unstructured time on their hands and contact with, or being influenced by antisocial peer groups. A high number have experimented with various forms of drugs or alcohol which in some cases means becoming dependent upon these substances. Many young people have long standing mental health problems and there are a significant number who have Attention Deficit Disorder. A high percentage have attempted self harm and/or had suicidal thoughts and many have attempted to act on these. Young people in secure units may present with one, some or all of these problems in any combination, with varying degrees of severity and differences in age of onset.

(Rose 2002: 33)

Given the previous experiences of children and young people in secure accommodation, it might be thought that the regimes of all institutions charged with their care and education would be focused on the provision of rehabilitative programmes and be based on credible theoretical models. It might also be presupposed that the support and training offered to the different professional groups who work in such establishments would be geared towards providing them with the knowledge and skills to meet the needs of the young people in their care. Similarly, it would not be too surprising if the management task in such settings included a substantial element of offering support to staff to help them understand both the complex (and sometimes bewildering) dynamics that exist in such environments and the impact on their own thoughts and feelings. Perhaps it is rather unsurprising that none of this is the case, and that despite the work of the Youth Justice Board over the past ten years, there is still not a coherent practice model for staff working in the secure estate.

Secure Training Centres (STCs) are the most recent type of secure unit for young people and were intended as something of a bridge between Secure Children's Homes and Young Offender Institutions. It is their management arrangements that are of particular interest for our present discussion:

The four Secure Training Centres, (STCs) are privately owned, built and run to specific contract specifications set out by the Youth Justice Board. They are smaller than the establishments within the prison service estate, ranging from 40–80 places. The Centres provide places for both boys and girls and there is a dedicated unit for mothers and babies at one Centre.

The ownership of these Centres is highly complex and has changed over the years as a result of various mergers and takeovers amongst the larger companies of which the STCs are subsidiaries. The "parent" companies have diverse service portfolios across a range of security, penal and related areas of work. The nature of the contract arrangements vary across the different STCs and the focus of external management is pretty much driven by the need to ensure compliance with the specific demands of the contract. As achieving compliance has financial implications in terms of possible penalties this plays a significant part in the prioritising of issues.

(Rose J in Blyth M, et al. 2008: 26)

The final sentences from the quotation reflect my actual experience as the director of one of these establishments in which the priority of the external management team was to implement a specific model of quality assurance. Implementing this model required detailed monitoring of how well staff followed standard procedures to ensure that the centre remained 'compliant' within the terms of its operational contract with the Youth Justice Board. In fact, very little else mattered. The most damaging effect of these rather crude mechanisms, also incidentally rather crudely enforced, was their constraining influence on staff and organisational development. All staff, including managers, were obliged to think in terms of compliance, rather than have ideas about their work or take advantage of opportunities to think about the young people for whom they were caring. And the young people who – because of their behaviour and occasionally bizarre presentation – were both puzzling and challenging to a largely inexperienced group of staff simply did not receive the kind of attention that they required.

The concept of 'compliance', much used in contemporary descriptions of organisational relationships, is not particularly appropriate when carried over as a descriptor for evaluating the routine daily life of an organisation whose purpose is to care for children and young people. For abused children, the idea of compliance resonates all too painfully with the kind of relationships into which they were forced by their adult abusers. This is an example of what happens when policy 'speak' becomes fused with the actual experiences of children and young people. Of course, the organisational rationale is that the two aspects are totally unrelated, i.e. there is a difference between how an organisation manages and talks about its work, and how the front line staff talk with the 'clients' – in this case children and young people. Yes, there is a gap! The problem is that in reality, there is no gap; there is a strong dynamic between organisational life and the direct work of the staff with their clients. It is a dynamic within which potent and sometimes unconscious processes operate, influencing feelings and behaviour in ways that affect not only the immediate organisation but the wider systems within which they operate as well.

RELATING AND THINKING

In the above paragraphs, I have tried to explore some of the underlying and contributing factors that shape the 'pervading culture' within which professionals have to work and which serve to constrain the way in which they are able to think about and carry on with their daily activities. In a culture where the declared priorities are to reach targets and maintain compliance, the value placed on thinking and reflection is minimal; the task is to deliver outcomes and achieve outputs.

The restriction that this approach imposes on those responsible for actually doing the work creates the need for a professional persona of competence and authority, which emphasises control and compliance, leading to risk aversive decision-making and sterility in interpersonal relationships. We will see in later chapters some of the specific effects of this on practice, and we will examine in more detail the ways in which rather than making children and young people safer and creating environments for healthy development and growth, the opposite is actually the case.

However, it is important to recognise that the processes already discussed are not necessarily bad or destructive in themselves. It is surely right that in instances where large amounts of public money are spent, there should be ways of evaluating how effectively the money is being used. It is also the case that not all aspects of professionalisation are unhelpful. Foster carers, for example, clearly benefit from training and supervision, and they are entitled to reasonable remuneration for the work they do and deserve a greater recognition for their contribution to the care of children and young people whose own families are unable to provide appropriate care for whatever reasons.

The point is that those tools and mechanisms, intended for monitoring or evaluating services, have become ends in themselves; the gathering of information, the business of auditing or of being compliant with procedural requirements, have become purpose rather than means. I well remember working in a local authority and having the sense that attendance at meetings was, for a good number of people, the 'job', i.e. the place where they fulfilled their professional responsibilities. Somehow, direct or face-to-face work was a secondary activity. The irony was that these meetings had to continue in perpetuity, because either the right people were not present for any definite decision to be taken, or decisions had to be referred and ratified at another meeting!

The function of 'quality assurance' as a defence against overwhelming anxiety is also the underlying purpose of the 'meeting syndrome', and it accounts for much of the blanket of regulation and procedure that hangs over the current organisational activity in our welfare-, educational and health services.

What we appear to be lacking at present are ways of reckoning the human qualities and experiences located in the matrix of relationships that make up daily life. If we want our welfare systems, health-education systems, and even our criminal-justice systems to provide conditions in which children and young people are safe, secure, and have the best opportunities for healthy development; then we need to achieve a shift towards making relational approaches the fulcrum for the design of these systems, as well as for the design of proper training and support systems for the workers within them. We now possess an ever-increasing knowledge base about the sorts of experiences that all children from an early age need for their healthy physical and emotional growth – and for the proper development of their cognitive functions. This knowledge base strongly supports the idea that relational approaches are the key to effective interventions and to achieving positive outcomes for children and families.

If the model for shaping and focusing work with children, young people and families is relational, then this too must be the priority of the wider-policy framework that directs organisations and shapes practice. In the same way, the structures and support systems within those organisations must be geared towards providing staff with levels of supervision and training that equip them thoroughly for their demanding work. In subsequent chapters, we shall see the implications of this approach not only for practitioners and managers, but also for those responsible for their education and training programmes and for wider policy formation.

Whilst the focus of this book is on human services and their specific organisation, the issues raised are inevitably of a wider and more general nature. They are to do with the kind of society in which we live, and the values that we wish to foster and use to shape our daily lives. The attention and care we give to our children and young people – and the resources we dedicate to their education and development – are indeed tests of what sort of society we are and what we aspire to be. The ideas of attachment and nurture, which we shall be thinking about, raise important questions that go to the very heart of what it means to be human. They challenge how we think about ourselves and how we build our lives as individuals, families and communities.

Chapter 3

Teaching self-esteem?

The calm existence that is mine
When I am worthy of myself

(William Wordsworth, *The Prelude*)

By studying neglect and its life altering consequences, Harlow con-
firmed love's central role in shaping not only how we feel but how we
think. The more children experience affection, the more curious they
become about the world.

(Deborah Blum, *Love at Goon Park*)

WELL-BEING AND GROWING UP WELL

If you were asked to list the main priorities for children's and family services, you probably would not include Harry Harlow's ideas about the central and shaping role of love! Neither, I suspect, would you refer to what reads like Wordsworth's definition of self-esteem? Your reply would be most likely to include data collection, target setting, performance measures, audit and inspection, short-term interventions, and the quest for measurable outcomes. It might well depend on your age whether or not your answer would include reference to the development of key skills; for example, thinking and reflection. These are certainly not at the top of the list in terms of their perceived importance for the majority of education and training programmes for professional workers.

However, almost paradoxically, over recent years there has been another strong thread running through central-policy statements regarding children and families. This thread encompasses the idea of 'well-being', which in this context is linked to providing the necessary conditions for children's healthy growth and development in a family setting.

The concept of well-being is not a new one; there is a long history of the idea in the study of philosophy, specifically ethics; and it is now linked to ideas about the psychology of happiness. It also touches crucially on the notion of welfarism.

> *Well-being is most commonly used in philosophy to describe what is non-instrumentally or ultimately good for a person. The question of what well-being consists in is of independent interest, but it is of great importance in moral philosophy, especially in the case of utilitarianism, according to which well-being is to be maximized. It has become standard to distinguish theories of well-being as either hedonist theories, desire theories, or objective list theories. According to the view known as welfarism, well-being is the only value. Also important in ethics is the question of how a person's moral character relates to their well-being.*

(Stanford Encyclopaedia of Philosophy 2008 'Well-Being')

The link here is to our earlier discussion about the impact that the present day emphasis on social control has on the way welfare-, health- and education-services are provided. The central question being: who decides what is in the best interest for whom? In particular, what secures the well-being of infants, children and young people – and on what principles do we base social policies in these critical areas? In 2008, the Children's Society published their report 'A Good Childhood'. The ambitious aims of the inquiry were '*to renew society's understanding of modern childhood and to inform, improve and inspire all our relationships with children.*' Evidence was contributed by over 30,000 people, including over 20,000 children who took part in polls as well as in research and focus groups. '*The research was far reaching and included children from all walks of life including children in prison, children in pupil referral units, children in early-years settings, refugee children, disabled children and many other marginalised groups*' (The Children's Society 2008). The final report reached a number of key conclusions, but central to its findings was the statement that:

Most of the obstacles children face today are linked to the belief among adults that the prime duty of the individual is to make the most of their own life, rather than contribute to the good of others ... excessive individualism is causing a range of problems for children including: high family break-up, teenage unkindness, commercial pressures towards premature sexualisation, unprincipled advertising, too much competition in education and acceptance of income inequality.

The conclusions of this report confirm the continuing relevance of certain ideas about relationships and mutuality, i.e. the importance of behaving in ways that are not just for the benefit of the individual, but for the individual in the context of others. These ideas about the reciprocal benefits enjoyed through relationships are central to the true meaning of well-being. In many respects, these findings echo research by Richard Alexander of Cambridge

University who – in the report of the '*Primary Review*', which was a three-year study into the state of primary education in England – found evidence that the current emphasis on exams and league tables has put increasing pressure on children in schools, whilst outside the classroom stress on children is increased by such factors as 'consumerism, the cult of celebrity and a desire to grow up too quickly.'

Every Child Matters is the central, major policy statement of recent years from which pretty much all other policy lines have emerged. The identified five outcomes of the policy are posited towards the well-being for every child and young person. As the Department for Children, Schools and Families (DCSF) website explains:

> *Every Child Matters is a strong national vision that drives the whole Change for Children programme. This is that children and young people can all achieve the five outcomes that they have told us are key to well-being in childhood and later life: being healthy, staying safe, enjoying and achieving, making a positive contribution and achieving economic well-being.*

Our shared ambition is to improve those outcomes for all children and to narrow the gap in outcomes between those who do well and those who do not. This overarching vision will be translated by local services into meaningful aims and objectives to meet the needs of children and young people in your area.

Whilst there are programmes and projects that espouse the principles of well-being for children, young people and their families; the fact remains that in the real world of work – be that social care, education, health or youth justice – many managers and practitioners do not feel that they are working within a policy framework or for organisations that support the achievement of these outcomes. Rather, they feel ensnared in a culture preoccupied with performance measurement and bureaucracy. This presents a serious conflict for managers and workers who are constantly called upon to make decisions about which of the competing items on their agendas at any one time they are going to prioritise.

CONFLICTING AGENDAS – A SCHOOL EXAMPLE

In one school in London, there was a very effective nurture group. As in most schools with nurture groups, this particular way of working with children had influenced the practices, behaviour and attitudes of the teaching staff across the whole school. The school, in a mixed inner-city area with its fair share of social problems and families needing additional support and help, also covered a wider catchment area of middle-class families who were ambitious for their children's academic success. The head teacher was under pressure to drive up standards and for her school to be seen competing in the local league tables, thus attracting a consistently high level of applications and intake numbers. With an impending Ofsted inspection, she clearly felt that a special effort was needed to ensure that the school received the highest grade possible. So she issued the instruction: 'Don't spend all that time talking to the children; just concentrate on their work.'

I suppose 'talking to the children' might have been her way of summing up the relational approach to learning, which is familiar in nurture groups; whilst their 'work' was the serious business that her staff needed to concentrate their efforts upon, and which would ultimately bring success to the school in the forthcoming inspection. We shall explore later the fallacy of the argument that seeks to split the process of learning in this way. The point here is that the head chose the item of the agenda that she thought she needed to prioritise in order to satisfy the demands of an inspection, i.e. performance and attainment. It requires brave and independent head teachers and senior managers of other services to stand against this tide. Holding together performance and nurture is challenging, but as we shall see, it is essential if children and young people are to successfully achieve and enjoy any sense of well-being in their formative years.

CONFLICTING AGENDAS – THINKING ABOUT THE REASONS

So, how might we think about the reasons for this conflict of agendas? Firstly, the drive for performance predominates because it is the fundamental mindset that directs the formulation of policy, and it is from this that the measures to achieve specific objectives emanate, inevitably influencing and shaping core organisational activities. Professional practice that draws upon what we might describe as the principles and ideas of relational or nurturing approaches is not regarded as sufficiently 'rigorous', yet alone it is sufficient to be the main foundation for policy formulation and service delivery.

Secondly, and perhaps more controversially, a case might be made that rather than being a catalyst for policy and practice development, any perceived emphasis on well-being is more of a response to the ever-growing and undeniable concerns about the extent of the problems identified in the mental health and high levels of anti-social behaviour amongst children and young people.

The irony is that if the connections were made between the way children learn and develop emotionally with how they learn and develop cognitively, then a more complete and holistic framework for both policy and practice would have the opportunity to emerge. This would address the concerns of all interested parties. In order for this to happen, however, the mindset needs to change. There is also a further irony in that this change of mindset would be wholly consistent with what 'science' is telling us about the needs of children in families and with our growing knowledge about what is essential and required for healthy growth and well-being!

As we shall see, ideas from attachment theory and the principles of nurture offer not just models for therapeutic work but models for thinking about and organising education and welfare services in ways that would bring benefit to all children. As Marion Bennathan, one of the main and original exponents of nurture groups has written:

> *Nurture groups can change children's lives. If all schools were run on nurturing principles, the long term benefits to children and to society would be immense.*

> (Nurture Group Network Individual Membership Form)

HOW WELL ARE OUR CHILDREN?

In recent years there has been growing concern about the increased morbidity rates in the mental health of children and young people. This has been linked in the priorities of central policy making to other issues, including teenage pregnancy, alcohol and substance abuse amongst young people, adolescent suicide rates and anti-social behaviour.

In addition, in a number of studies widely publicised in the national media, British children have been designated as amongst the unhappiest and least well adjusted in Europe. The following statistics indicate the scale of the problems:

- Of children and young people in the UK, 20% have mental health problems at some point, and one in ten has a clinically recognisable mental health disorder.

- Up to one in 12 British children deliberately hurt themselves on a regular basis – the highest rate in Europe.

- Between 1972 and 2004, the proportion of children in the UK living in single-parent families more than tripled to 24%.

A study of children's well-being in 25 European countries ranked the UK in 21st place. The UK scored badly for relationships with parents and peers, child health, relative poverty, deprivation and risky behaviour, including cigarette smoking, drunkenness, and cannabis use, teenage pregnancy, unsafe sexual intercourse and on children's evaluation of their happiness and health. (Child and Adolescent Mental Health Services, Mental Health Foundation Summerfield and Gill, UNICEF)

It would not be right, however, to reproduce these statistics without reference to the counter views offered to those who portray current experiences of childhood in the bleakest of terms. Such opposing views tend to express concerns about childhood being a consequence of adult anxieties and the increasingly risk-averse nature of modern living.

Tim Gill, former director of the UK Children's Play Council and author of *No Fear: Growing Up in a Risk Averse Society*, published by the Caloustie Gulbenkian Foundation (2007), has commented, '*Over the past 30 years, activities that previous generations of children have enjoyed without a second thought have been relabelled as troubling or dangerous, and the adults who permit them branded as irresponsible. Childhood is being undermined by adults' increasing aversion to risk and by the intrusion of that fear into every aspect of their lives. The knock-on effect is extremely serious.*'

I take up the specific issues of risk and the management of associated anxieties in later chapters in considering their effect on a number of contentious issues that arise in situations of direct practice. At this point, the assessment and management of risk forms part of the background to the widespread expression of concerns about a number of negative factors affecting childhood in contemporary society. These factors are deemed to influence significantly what it is like to be growing up today and to have serious implications for the health, education and general well-being of all children.

It is one of the themes of this book that anxieties about risk – and the associated fear of what may happen if things go wrong – contribute to the pressures on adults who work in social care and education. These pressures are yet another destructive aspect of what we have described as the predominating culture for the development of policy, the delivery of services and the education of the professional workforce.

NURTURE GROUPS AND THE SOCIAL AND EMOTIONAL ASPECTS OF LEARNING

Nurture groups, along with the principles and ideas upon which they are based, provide an important model not just for work with children, young people and families in schools, but for wider application across all services. With their origin in the work of an educational psychologist, the late Marjorie Boxall, and a history stretching back over 40 years, nurture groups are a well-tried and proven intervention, developed in many respects way ahead of their time in terms of the acceptance of their key principles across education practice in schools. What is encouraging now is the way in which these principles have influenced programmes such as the Social and Emotional Aspects of Learning (SEAL), which has become part of the curriculum in primary and secondary schools across England and Wales.

In Aspects of Social and Emotional Learning in the United Kingdom, Christopher Clouder and Belinda Heys sketch the background to the SEAL initiative and confirm the range of concerns that generated interest for its development. Clouder and Heys link the programme with a growing realisation about the limitations of current education philosophy and its emphasis on testing and targets.

> *Over the years more emphasis has been placed on testing as a way of improving standards and now it is reckoned that children in England take a high-profile test or exam virtually every year of their school career, the highest figure in the world. There is a strengthening reaction to the never-ending testing culture among teachers, their unions and educators in general, so both the prescriptions of the national curriculum and the amount of testing attached to them are gradually being eased. This practice of continuous summative assessment by testing is seen, in some quarters, as a source of stress and is known to its critics as 'education by numbers'.*

(Clouder and Heys 2008: 46)

The link between emotional well-being and children's ability to learn is acknowledged in the SEAL curriculum, and its relevance to the development of positive, pro-social behaviour, compliance and performance management does not go unnoticed!

> *The Secretary of State for Children, School and Families, a high ranking ministerial post, announced officially (in August 2007) that all state schools in England will be given the opportunity to be supported to develop the social and emotional skills of all their pupils, using the Social and Emotional Aspects of Learning (SEAL) programme as the vehicle for this. SEAL is described as a comprehensive approach to promoting social and emotional skills that underpin effective learn-*

*ing, positive behaviour, regular attendance, staff effectiveness and the
emotional health and well-being of all who learn and work in schools.*

(ibid. 47)

SEAL materials were initially introduced in primary schools, but they have
now been extended to make them relevant for use with older pupils. This par-
allels recent developments in the way nurture groups have been established
in secondary schools and other settings for adolescents. Clouder and Heys
indicate the sorts of difficulties that may arise when these approaches are introduced into these settings,. These difficulties include the larger number of
staff who need to be convinced of the value of such approaches and actively
encouraged to become involved in their implementation; the increased pressure at secondary level to achieve successful examination results ;and the tradition of subject-focused teaching rather than approaches that concentrate
on pupils' wider, developmental needs.

Another crucial aim for the introduction of the SEAL programme was that it
should not be seen simply as a programme to be delivered in classrooms, but
rather *'it would provide a framework and guidance to support schools to develop
pupils' social and emotional skills within each school's unique setting'* (ibid: 51).
The importance of a whole school approach and the creation of a culture or
ethos in which the values of social and emotional well-being can be fostered
also resonates with the nurture group experience and the research findings
about the impact of nurture groups on the general school and wider communities (Cooper 2007).

Professor Katherine Weare of the University of Southampton has written
extensively about these matters, and Clouder and Heys quote from her meta-
analysis of the main, systematic reviews of research in this area. Professor
Weare lists the necessary features of successful programmes that aim to support emotional and social learning as follows:

- They include explicit teaching and learning programmes that develop
  key skills, attitudes and behaviours, in pupils and staff

- They take a whole school approach and link with existing work in
  schools, including and especially on the promotion of good behaviour and sound learning

- They involve parents and the community

- They are supported by outside agencies, working together in a coordinated and coherent way

• They are coherent and well planned

• They last for many years, and do not expect instant results

• They start early, in the primary or even infant school

• They encourage appropriate climates that foster warm relationships, encourage participation, develop pupil and teacher autonomy, and foster clarity about boundaries, rules and positive expectations

• They promote teachers' emotional and social competence and well-being, and provide appropriate staff development

(Clouder and Heys op cit: 51)

In drawing this together, Clouder and Heys summarise:

> *The policy that SEAL represents is not a prescriptive programme that can be manufactured, duplicated and then imitated across institutions or cultures, but an ongoing process of development.*

(Clouder and Heys op cit: 52)

The aims of such programmes as SEAL are clearly laudable. The question is to what extent have the wider aims for such programmes – in which the ideas that underpin social and emotional development are not just taught as part of a curriculum but influence wider policy – been achieved or to what extent have they influenced the setting of priorities for children's services, including youth justice?

Professor Weare's list is a useful starting point in identifying the important features that must be applied when trying to build upon the fundamental ideas previously described (such as nurturing or relational approaches) in the creation of a robust framework for policy and practice. This framework must be strong enough to support not only individual therapeutic work, but also the organisation and management of services. We shall look at this in more detail in the next chapter.

ATTACHMENT MATTERS

In recent years, there has been a dramatic growth in the amount and availability of information and materials regarding attachment theory. There is no need to restate details of the theory here, as they can be read in the extensive literature on the subject, although we do need to remind ourselves of the main points. The 'References and Suggestions for Further Reading' section at the end of this book indicates some of the main work that it is important and necessary to read in order to understand attachment theory – and in particular to see the relevance of recent research in the areas of neuroscience and brain development.

The interest here is in understanding the significance of attachment and infant-brain development and how they are connected to the approaches and organisation of early-years family support, education, social care and related services and institutions. If attachment and nurturing are of such significance, why are these ideas not the main influencing knowledge and evidence-base for policy and practice, and similarly, why are they not used as core material for the education and training of the children's workforce?

Clouder and Heys pose the question as to whether there will be a continuing financial investment in similar approaches to the SEAL initiative; but perhaps more importantly, they also point out that:

> *The danger is that SEAL, and other such endeavours too, will fall victim to the prevalent target-setting measures, as has been already mooted for creativity in schools. Much remains to be done and advocates of this approach have a formidable task ahead of them. The "delivery" model of education is deeply entrenched and in spite of its well-documented shortcomings will take much effort to be transformed into a more child-orientated approach.*

(Clouder and Heys op cit: 77)

The outstanding challenge is to influence the wider, political context where the decision-making processes are based and policy priorities are determined. As has been pointed out earlier in this chapter, even by applying the current criteria for what constitutes evidence results in a strong and growing body of knowledge that supports and affirms that by addressing the emotional and social development needs of children, improvements in their school attendance, behaviour and academic attainments will follow. Why should this be so?

IDEAS FROM ATTACHMENT

Attachment behaviours are common to all mammals. We are now very famil-iar with the image of baby ducklings walking in line, following their mother and seeking proximity for their protection and food. These are behaviours that typify early experiences of mothers and babies in the animal world. Without the protective behaviours of their mother and other adults, baby mammals cannot survive; either they fall victim to a predator or they starve. The length of time that this dependency lasts is variable, but it is always a crucial period and determines rates of survival into adulthood.

For human infants similar principles apply, but there are qualitative dif-ferences in the nature of the relationship between a human infant and its mother. These differences distinguish our humanity and are significant for later development and growth. Robin Balbernie describes these qualitative differences as intersubjectivity, which is *'uniquely human, a shared experience of interacting emotional worlds. This is the overlap where mother and baby pro-duce a felt event in common; when they actively participate in and influence each other's feelings. It is what occurs within this space, set up by the biological force of attachment and enhanced by mirror neurons, that influences future social, emo-tional and neurological development.'* (Balbernie 2007).

It is the quality of this early relationship that significantly influences the processes of later growth and development. It is the linking of the 'biologi-cal force of attachment' with the physiological and chemical reactions of the brain that create the conditions for the unique development of each child and that set the scene for how that child will grow and develop; emotionally, psychologically and socially. What research teaches us is that babies are born with an innate ability to relate to others in the world around them.

> It is now clear that 'the infant comes to the world with a biological preparedness for participating in social interactions...The infant has built-in capacities for initiating, maintaining, and terminating social interactions with others.
>
> (Sameroff and Emde 1989 :38)

It is through a relationship with their primary care giver, usually the mother, that a child's early learning takes place. These experiences provide the con-text for all later learning. Fundamentally, what the child learns through this primary relationship are the answers to questions: Is the world a safe place for me? Can I rely on this person and other adults to look after me? Will my needs be met when I need them to be? Will there always be someone there for me when I need protection? The answers that a child receives to these questions within the early days, months and years of infancy lead to the formation of what John Bowlby referred to as their 'internal working model', i.e. a view based on their experience of how safe the world is and what their place in it is likely to be. In what has been described as the first-year attachment-cycle, a baby learns that needs can be met and anxieties contained through the protective, providing, caring and soothing responses of their mother, who either provides an immediate response to the expressed needs, or attends to them within a sufficiently short enough time. This experience is the basis for the formation of a secure attachment between a mother and her baby – a relationship which is crucial for later development and which will significantly influence the child's capacity for learning.

From a very early age, an infant begins to develop behaviours and strategies that help them respond happily when positive behaviour is shown towards them. In adverse circumstances, however, they will also develop responses to ensure their survival in hostile, unsafe and uncaring environments. Both sets of behaviour are developed based on their experience of the world around them and, most significantly, as a result of the way the adults in that world act towards them.

In those uncaring situations, when an infant's increasingly defensive behaviour interacts with the inconsistent, neglectful or hostile offerings of care by the adult, the formation of an attachment relationship is far from secure and it will develop along the lines of one of the defined categories of insecure attachment relationships. The particular presentation of an insecure attachment varies according to the specific relational experiences between the infant and their care giver. The degree, frequency, and extent of any neglect or abuse affect a child's responses to their situation and shape the way in which their behaviour manifests the disturbed-attachment experience.

In general terms, the 'internal working model' of an insecurely attached child suffers distortion and is characterised by feelings of low self-worth, the inability to receive praise or criticism, a suspicion and hostility to new experiences, a lack of trust in adults, and difficulties in making and sustaining relationships. Such feelings and their associated behavioural responses – which are designed to defend against a dangerous, external world – inevitably lead to difficulties for a child in negotiating the normal tasks of childhood, such as starting school or making new friends. The experiences of those early years, positive and negative, continue to play a formative role throughout childhood, into adolescence and right throughout the life span.

ATTACHMENT AND ADOLESCENCE

The growing interest in nurture groups and similar interventions in secondary schools and other settings that work with young people is testimony to the increasing awareness of the importance of attachment issues for adolescence.

As we shall see, recent advances in neuroscience have particular relevance for work with adolescents; they have greatly enhanced our knowledge about the opportunities for further development and reparation that arise during these years.

This is important when we realise that a good number of government policies and the resources that flow with them are directed towards trying to find solutions to the problems that a proportion of young people present to wider society. We must remember as well that it is in adolescence that issues of mental health, anti-social behaviour and criminality begin to emerge and make an impact, and concerns such as youth crime or levels of teenage pregnancy are always high profile and of public interest. Central government and wider public concern is not only focused on delinquent behaviour; witness the pressures on mainstream schools to perform well and for their pupils to achieve successful examination results.

Underpinning this increasing interest in the adolescent population are the financial implications of having to deal with the consequences of anti-social behaviour. Not the least of these is a result of the very high rate of incarceration for young offenders – a virulent example of the way our particular youth justice system operates (Rob Allen in Blyth et al. 2008: 35ff). It is also part of a wider social perspective that with an ageing national population, a huge welfare-benefits bill and the increased costs and expectations on health-care services, it is essential to have as competent and large a workforce as possible earning money to support the growing demands on the public purse. It is surely not a coincidence that 'making a contribution' and 'economic well-being' are two out of the five outcomes required for all children in the *Every Child Matters* programme!

Given what we know about the effectiveness of early years' preventative work and the huge costs of interventions in later years, why has there not been a more whole-hearted switch to preventative and early support services? Although many different types of resources have been put into early prevention strategies, the mindsets that direct policy and provide for its implementation have not really changed, as evidenced by the problems associated with the conflict of agendas previously outlined.

The importance of secure attachment in infancy and the long-term consequences of poor early years learning experiences are now in many respects no brainers!

Even with the difficult and entrenched problems associated with adolescence, the ideas of attachment and the powerful, ameliorating effects of nurturing practices have been shown to make significant differences to the lives of young people and have enhanced their opportunities into adulthood.

LEARNING FROM NEUROSCIENCE

Advances in neuroscience and in particular the improved technology of scanning, which allows observers to see the activity and processes that contribute to healthy brain development, have revolutionised our knowledge and understanding of how the infant brain grows. The idea of nurturing can no longer be dismissed as a rather woolly concept that belongs in the nursery rather than in the hardnosed world of objective science! Now we know about the biochemistry of nurture: the complex relationship in how the brain of a new born baby grows and develops in correlation to the quality of the nurturing it receives from its primary carer – most especially the mother.

These early experiences are the foundation for secure attachment and provide the essential building blocks of learning, which then shape the template for later relationships and behaviour. There is a sequential pattern to how the brain grows; the basic needs of an infant, for protection and survival, are provided for within the context of the early attachment relationship, and the development of the primitive brain is structured to ensure this need is met. It is upon this basis – and through the nurturing power of a continuing, consistent and secure attachment relationship – that higher-level brain development takes place. Successful development at this level, which includes such functions as the regulation of emotions, the emergence of empathy, and the higher cognitive processes, is a further outcome of secure attachment.

It is now established that as brain development continues into adolescence, this particular stage provides another window in which growth can be encouraged through positive and affirming relationships with adults. The notion of learning through relationships is not confined to the baby and infant. And this is the really good news: early damage through insecure attachment is not irreparable. The nature and quality of subsequent relationships and experiences make a difference. Of course, there are issues of degree and extent for both damage and repair; but the contention is that even into adolescence, the experience of having relationships with adults that provide the right ingredients to support development can bring about changes.

ATTACHMENT AND POLICY – LOOKING AHEAD

The significance of the above discussion extends beyond providing pointers for individual intervention, however important that may be for particular children, young people and their families. Neither should these ideas be limited to influencing the planning and structure of services for the early years.

Given the framework of knowledge this understanding about human development gives us, it has an undeniably important role in becoming the main source from which we draw all the policy lines for children, young people and families. This, in turn, will influence how the delivery of services is organised and managed and will contribute in a defining way to the content and ethos of education and training programmes for the professional workforce.

Chapter 4

'Growth Not Pathology'

An understanding heart is everything in a teacher, and cannot be esteemed highly enough. One looks back with appreciation to the brilliant teachers, but with gratitude to those who touched our human feeling. The curriculum is so much necessary raw material, but warmth is the vital element for the growing plant and for the soul of the child.

Carl Jung (1875–1961)

Marjorie Boxall coined the wonderfully evocative phrase 'growth not pathology' (Boxall 2002:10) to describe the way of thinking about children embodied by nurture groups. Currently over a thousand schools across the United Kingdom benefit from having nurture groups and can bear testimony to how this intervention, based on ideas from attachment theory and with a vital recognition of the importance of early learning experiences, has made a difference not just to individual children but to their families, their schools and their wider communities.

It is said of the late Marjorie Boxall, who developed the original model of nurture groups, that she had little time for 'theory' or for theorising. In her work as a beleaguered educational psychologist in Inner London in the late 1960s, she realised that showing affection or 'nurturing' was a natural, instinctive response to the immediate and obvious needs of the children in the classrooms of schools she visited. Carrying a child around in her arms, pointing out interesting pictures on the walls, or giving time and attention to the particular needs of a distressed child, seemed to her the true basis for encouraging learning. Responding to the needs of a child as appropriate to their presenting developmental stage – rather than in an arbitrary way linked to expectations of chronological attainment – made more sense and produced better results! The phrase 'growth not pathology' emphasises the nature of the children's difficulties as having their origins in poor experiences, rather than in some diagnosable or inherent disorder. It is this premise that we shall explore later when thinking about the wider application of the principles of nurture in areas such as social care and youth justice.

In effect, what Marjorie Boxall was so cleverly representing in the emerging practice of nurture groups were the principles of attachment theory applied to an educational setting. Over the past 40 years, we have come to know more about the importance of early attachment relationships in determining the way children respond to the world around them, and about how they develop patterns of behaviour to cope with whatever life may throw at them. We also know more about the biochemical, neurological correlation between the quality of these relationships and the physiological growth of the brain. As Marjorie Boxall might have put it, this looks very much like 'science catching up with common sense'. Or, to express it another way, it is scientific confirmation that those naturally intuitive things parents have done for their babies for generations – picking them up and holding them, smiling at them, responding to their cries, playing 'peek-a-boo' games, and generally fussing over them – are crucial elements for ensuring a baby's healthy emotional and physical growth.

Her own definition of attachment, although she may not have recognised it as such, is marvellously comprehensive:

> Satisfactory emotional, social and cognitive development in the earliest years is the product of adequate and attentive early nurturing care. It's a many-stranded, intermeshing, forward-moving, unitary learning process that centres on attachment and trust, and has its foundations in the close identification of parent and child, and the interaction and participation in shared experiences that stem from this.

(Bennathan and Boxall 2000: 22)

Whilst there is recognition that programmes such as SEAL need to be providing more than just materials for lessons in schools, the context in which these materials are currently used predicates that all too often this becomes the case. In the best instances, as shown by Clouder and Heys, the use of these materials to reinforce the development of a broader school ethos, incorporating a general recognition of the importance of emotional well-being as the basis of learning for all pupils, can be very effective. The question remains, however, as to what extent this can be achieved in a policy environment that prioritises performance and achievement and measures these by narrow and constraining indicators?

The defining factor for the effectiveness of nurture groups at overcoming children's barriers to learning is the set of experiences that the children enjoy through their relationships with the adults leading the group. The activities of the group are important, but they are essentially the pegs upon which hangs the main, therapeutic activity, i.e. the development of a trusting and nurturing relationship that sensitively and thoughtfully addresses the gaps identified in each individual child's early learning experience.

HOW NURTURE GROUPS BEGAN

Nurture groups are not new. Marjorie Boxall encountered large numbers of young children who were entering primary school with severe emotional, behavioural and social difficulties, leading to unmanageable rates of referral for placement in special schools or for child-guidance treatment. She understood the difficulties presented by most of these children as the outcome of impoverished early nurturing. Lacking an adequate experience of being cherished and attended to, they were not able to make trusting relationships with adults or respond appropriately to other children. They were unready to meet the social and intellectual demands of school life, a failure that further compounded the damage to their already fragile self-confidence and self-esteem.

In response to this situation, Marjorie Boxall developed the model of 'nurture groups'. Because the children remained a part of their base class by registering there in the morning and returning for the last part of the afternoon, the group was in no way stigmatising or excluding. The whole school were informed of the purpose of the group and were trained to give support; base-class teachers sent the child off with the group teacher or assistant to have a good day, and then greeted them with interest on their return. The reputation of the groups was so high that other children wanted to join them and most schools devised schemes for allowing this, such as invitations to tea, or sharing story-time.

Through the 1970s, the groups spread rapidly in Inner London and elsewhere in the UK, largely by word of mouth, and quickly gained official approval. In 1978, the influential Warnock Report stated:

> Among compensatory measures which may be taken we have been impressed by the 'nurture groups' which have been started in a number of primary schools in London for children approaching or over the age of five who are socially and emotionally affected by severe deprivation in early childhood.

(Warnock 1978 Para 5.30).

By the mid-1980s, the Inner London Education Authority (ILEA) was taking a lead in the national move towards inclusive education by setting up a committee headed by their Chief Inspector, John Fish. The head teachers of the 50 or more schools, which had nurture groups, were in no doubt that the groups were central to successful inclusion and made strong recommendations of which the committee took note. Its report 'Educational Opportunities For All?' widely acclaimed nationally, stated:

> *The concept of nurture work ... for children who have not experienced many common domestic ... learning experiences, or whose stressful experiences have prevented them from profiting from them, is an important one. Much has been learned from this form of provision which could inform other special educational arrangements. Because it is based in schools, where the teachers work closely with others in the school it can help teachers of other classes gain insight and provide for children who might have special educational needs. As an approach with a clear rationale aimed at preventing many difficulties becoming special educational needs, it is to be endorsed.*

(Fish 1985)

The Greater London Council of which ILEA was part was abolished in 1989 and Marjorie Boxall, central to the training and support of nurture group staff, retired. The new Inner London Boroughs did not include nurture groups in their special education plans. While many schools held on to their nurture groups, there was no longer an incipient national focus.

THE GROWTH OF NURTURE GROUPS

The continuing support for nurture groups was provided by the Association of Workers for Children with Emotional and Behavioural Difficulties (AWCEBD), a long established charity, now rebranded as the Social Emotional and Behavioural Difficulties Association (SEBDA), whose continuing aim is to promote good practice in work with children with emotional and behavioural difficulties. The AWCEBD was deeply concerned by the likely effects of the 1988 Education Act on its client group. The Act – with its introduction of the National Curriculum and emphasis on raising attainments, assessment and publication of results, and parental choice of schools – seemed likely to make schools less tolerant of troubled and troublesome children. It was a matter of urgency to get nurture groups, which the association recognised as effective early intervention, back on the public agenda. In 1996, the book Effective Intervention in Primary Schools: Nurture Groups written by Marion Bennathan and Marjorie Boxall was published. It fixed nurture groups into the changing educational setting, drawing heavily on the experience of Enfield, an Outer London borough, where nurture groups had become part of the local education authority's special needs policy and were established within a framework of agreed procedures with assessed outcomes and annual audits.

In October 1997, The DfEE green paper *'Excellence for all Children: Meeting Special Educational Needs'* strongly advocated the education of pupils with special educational needs in mainstream school. The AWCEBD had drawn the government's attention to the relevance of nurture groups in terms of many aspects of policy: reducing exclusions, raising academic standards, increasing social inclusion by reducing truancy and improving behaviour. The green paper recognised that the 'one group which presents schools with special challenges (is) ... children with emotional and behavioural difficulties. The number of children perceived as falling within this group is increasing' (Green paper 1997: 77). The need for early identification and intervention was stressed, and nurture groups in Enfield were cited as the example of good practice:

> *In Enfield, some primary schools run nurture groups for children showing early signs of emotional and behavioural difficulties. These small special classes provide a structured and predictable environment in which the children can begin to trust adults and to learn. Careful consideration is given to appropriate curriculum content. The nurture groups are an integral part of Enfield schools' mainstream provision for children with special educational needs. The LEA's advisory staff and educational psychology service support and train the nurture group teachers and assistants. Parents are regularly involved in discussion about their child's progress and attend informal sessions. Pupils are encouraged to take part in school activities including assemblies and playtimes. Many pupils are able to function wholly within a mainstream class within a year.*

(ibid. 80)

The publication in 1998, *'Meeting Special Educational Needs: A Programme of Action'*, announced that: 'a national programme will be in place to help primary schools tackle emotional and behavioural difficulties at an early stage' (Document 1998: 44).

> *Primary nurture groups – we are supporting, in partnership with the University of Cambridge and the Association of Workers for Children with Emotional and Behavioural Difficulties, a research project to promote primary age nurture groups for children who on entry to school show the effects of inadequate early learning experiences. They offer an educational programme precisely structured to the emotional, social and intellectual needs of each pupil while keeping them in close contact with their normal class.*

The following year, the paper 'Social Inclusion: Pupil Support' (Document 1999) was issued by the DfES in collaboration with the Social Exclusion Unit (part of the Cabinet Office and central to a wide range of cross-departmental government policies), with the Home Office and with the Department of Health. The paper focused particularly on the need for regular attendance at school and for high standards of behaviour, and on reducing the level of unauthorised absences and exclusions. It acknowledged that some pupils are at particular risk of poor attendance or of exclusion, notably those with emotional and/or behavioural difficulties. Again, attention was drawn to the effective early intervention provided in Enfield by nurture groups:

> *Many of the children entering the school have a history of disrupted parenting and seriously under-developed social and linguistic skills that make participation in mainstream learning difficult. The small special classes provide a structured and predictable environment in which children can begin to trust adults and to learn.*

(ibid.11)

Nurture groups have continued to receive endorsement in official reports. The Steer reports (2004, 2009) on behaviour in schools have noted the positive impact made by nurture groups on children's behaviour and comment favourably on the training provided by the Nurture Group Network to support practitioners. More recently Ofsted (2009) noted the effect of nurture groups in reducing exclusions amongst very young children.

With well over a thousand groups across the United Kingdom, nurture groups have flourished in recent years and there is strong interest overseas as well, especially in Canada and New Zealand. Much of this progress has been a result of the work of the vibrant and growing umbrella organisation of the Nurture Group Network. The independent charity has utilised the knowledge and skills of its membership, and the enthusiastic and committed work of its trustees, to provide the necessary impetus and leadership for the development of nurture group practices. This has been achieved through a comprehensive national training programme, an accredited quality assurance award for nurture groups (the Marjorie Boxall Quality Mark Award), and the publication of resource materials for schools. The outcomes of an increasing body of evidence from both national and regional research studies support the claims made about nurture groups in terms of their effectiveness in helping children and their families, as well as their impact on the ethos of schools and their wider communities.

WHAT ARE NURTURE GROUPS?

In what have been traditionally described as 'classic' groups, now more commonly known as Boxall groups, nurture groups are classes of ten or so children set up in primary schools with their own room, preferably in a central part of the school. Each group is an integral part of a school's provision, understood and supported by all the staff.

Training for nurture group staff emphasises the importance of accepting and valuing each child and responding to them at whatever developmental stage they might have reached, whether they need comfort and physical contact like a baby, control like a two-year old in a tantrum stage, or repeated explanations like a three-year old at the 'why?' stage.

A standard day in a Boxall nurture group sees the group's children register with their 'base' class. Collected by group staff, these children spend most of their day in the special nurture group room, keeping in contact with the rest of the school by joining them for midday lunch and at playtime, and then returning to their 'base' class for the last part of the day. It is recommended that nurture group staff should have one afternoon session for recording and planning, training or for meetings with parents. On average, children spend up to four terms in the nurture group before re-joining their mainstream class.

In many schools there are variations on the above, usually in terms of the length of time spent in the group each day or by increasing involvement with their mainstream class in certain subject areas; but nurture groups always work to the core principles encapsulated in the above description, i.e.

- Children's learning is understood developmentally

- The classroom offers a safe base

- Nurture is essential for the development of self-esteem

- Language is a vital means of communication – more than a 'tool', it is a vehicle for expressing feelings and emotions

- All behaviour is communication

- Transitions are important in children's lives

These principles have evolved and been refined by the work of a number of key people over the years, in particular by Eva Holmes, formerly principal educational psychologist in the London Borough of Enfield. Along with operational characteristics required for effective practice, the principles encapsulate the ideas that provide for extended application into other areas of practice, as well as for the management and organisation of services. A form of the nurture group model was developed by education staff in one Young Offender Institution to such good effect that it was commended by the Prison Service Inspectorate, who noted the influence of the work in the group on other aspects of the regime (Bourne 2008). Nurture groups have also been adapted for residential special schools where the influence is not only on the 'school' part of the establishment, but also in the residential units.

THE BOXALL PROFILE

The Boxall Profile is the tool routinely used by nurture group staff to assess the suitability of children for placement in a group. Devised and developed by Marjorie Boxall and Marion Bennathan, the Boxall Profile is widely used in schools with nurture groups and has also proved a useful aid in schools without specific nurture group provision, where it helps staff think about the developmental needs of individual children. There is also experience in using the profile in other settings, such as Young Offender Institutions. The profile has been successfully used in secondary schools, although its standardisation is with children aged between 3½ years and 8 years of age. With the increasing interest in nurture groups and their effectiveness for older children, the Nurture Group Network has had the foresight to re-standardise the profile for use with this older age group and for easier use in alternative settings with young people.

Marion Bennathan and Martin Haskayne (the network's national training manager) outline the structure and main principles of the profile and indicate its usefulness for staff in an article 'The Effectiveness of the Boxall Profile', available through the Nurture Group Network website. One of the advantages of the profile is that the person using it does not require specific qualifications in psychology. Although there is a need for appropriate training in how to complete the profile – and most importantly, how to interpret the 'scores' of the assessment – teachers, support staff and other professionals who use it are quickly able to grasp the principles required for its application and to see the benefits and relevance to their work. Analysing the profile helps them to understand more about the developmental experiences of individual children and to make sense of their behaviour in the classroom or other settings. This increased insight leads to more focused work with both individuals and groups of children, and it allows for progress to be marked.

The usefulness of the profile for workers who know and work directly with children and young people is not only a particular strength of the profile, but reflects a vital feature of wider nurture group practice: nurture groups do not require experts to be 'parachuted' in to work their magic and then depart! The nurture group approach proclaims that front line staff are the 'experts'; they are the people who know the children best and who, with appropriate training and management support, are best placed to provide the most effective intervention. This gives credence to the possibilities for developing the use of the profile not just for schools, but for use in other settings as well. For example, the potential for foster carers, supported by social workers, to use an adapted profile to help them think about the children they are caring for is a very exciting prospect.

These two quotations (taken from the cover of the Boxall Profile Handbook) reflect the widespread appreciation of the value of the profile. They are the views of someone who teaches a class of six-year-olds, and the head of education in a residential special school for children with serious emotional and behavioural difficulties.

> 'Confronted with a child whose anxiety-provoking behaviour seems to make no sense, the Profile is where you start. It gives you insights and suggests points of entry into the child's world.'
> 'It is very easy to use, quick and constructive. It is only too easy for teachers to start labelling children as aggressive or psychopathic. The Profile makes people think about what lies behind the behaviour'.

MESSAGES FROM RESEARCH ABOUT NURTURE GROUPS

We have already thought about the innovative and creative approach taken by the Nurture Group Network in developing a comprehensive format for the evaluation of nurture groups. Since their inception, however, practice in nurture groups has included the collection and collation of information about individual children, and then this information has been used to help plan future intervention and to monitor progress. This is one of the main purposes of the Boxall Profile: even when a child has left the group, the continuing use of the profile maintains a record of how that child is progressing, so as they grow older staff can remain focused on their changing needs. This priority of monitoring and evaluating has been an integral part of all nurture group training provision in the on-campus university courses in London, Leicester and Cambridge as well as in the network's own courses around the country.

Two main research programmes for the evaluation of nurture groups have published their findings. The national research programme at the University of Leicester, lead by Paul Cooper and David Whitebread, was published in 2007; and the study of the successful introduction and development of nurture group provision in the city of Glasgow detailed its outcomes in a report to Glasgow City Council in February 2007.

Both of these reports are available at the Nurture Group Network website. They draw similar conclusions as to the overall value of nurture groups and as to the difference that nurture groups make to children's progress in school in terms of such criteria as attendance, behaviour in school and at home, and academic attainment. Of considerable interest are the common findings that indicate nurture groups make a substantial difference to both the overall ethos of a school and to the relationships that a school has with children's parents. Indeed, the comments and views of parents about nurture groups make them amongst their most powerful advocates (Bennathan, M. Rose, J. 2008).

APPLYING THE MODEL

With such a strong and growing body of evidence and information about nurture groups, there can be confidence in drawing upon the model for wider application. Nurture groups as such, however, are primarily a school-based intervention and in many important ways this is their great strength, especially given the generic nature of school attendance, which carries none of the stigma that may surround a family's involvement with social care, mental health or youth justice services. But that is not to conclude that the principles of nurture groups or the adaptations of the model cannot be taken into other areas of practice with families, children or young people.

Nurture groups provide an important example of how the ideas of attachment theory can be implemented in practice and also provide a template for the planning of provision for early years' services. The case for early intervention needs to be made continually and powerfully because the evidence is clear that it is in the child's early years that the potential for long-term positive change is greatest.

However, the principles that inform nurture group practice in both primary and secondary schools have a wider relevance for the services and agencies that respond to the needs of the most vulnerable and worrying children, young people and families. In addition, these principles provide pointers as to how the wider issues of policy direction and organisational structures might be more hopefully addressed. As we have previously argued, without changes in the 'mindset' of those who formulate policy, and without the enhanced development of organisational cultures to better support such very difficult work, nurturing practices will never become mainstream. The consequence of which is that the benefits associated with the applied principles of nurture may never be experienced by the most needy of children and families who urgently require it.

THE SIX PRINCIPLES OF NURTURE

• Children's learning is understood developmentally

The developmental approach taken in nurture groups is an important first step in refocusing the staff's view of the children with whom they are working.

In nurture groups, children are responded to 'as they are' in ways that are both non-judgmental and accepting. How often in conflict situations with young people have I heard the exasperated cry from a member of staff or a bewildered foster carer, 'He's nearly sixteen, but he's behaving like a five-year-old!' It is not always tactful to treat this like a 'eureka moment', but the point can be gently made later that this is indeed exactly what is happening. Responses to a frustrated and seemingly aggressive young person need to reflect the developmental perspective with which he or she is confronting the world around them. Of course, this is not easy; the babying of young people is not to be recommended and unlikely to meet with a positive response!

Gauging a sensitive reaction and using appropriate language to calm a potentially explosive situation requires skill and insight, and it invariably works best if it occurs within an already established and trusting relationship between an adult and a young person.

A developmental perspective also informs expectations about the capacity of a child or young person to behave in ways that conform to social norms. Whilst not excusing 'bad behaviour', it is of some help to understand that the raging adolescent in front of you is not only behaving in accordance with an earlier developmental stage (not yet successfully negotiated despite the passing of years), but that their brain is not yet sufficiently developed enough to regulate the chemically induced emotional charge brought about by the situation in which they find themselves. Of course, this does not ease the difficulty of managing the moment, but over time an increased understanding of both the sequential nature of human development and of the integral connection of emotional awareness with the physiological development of the brain provides a backcloth against which better and more effective practice can emerge.

Some concession to this viewpoint has been made recently with announce-ments to do with the introduction of 'personal education' and a move away from statutory testing on an age basis. The recognition that 'children develop at different rates' seems to have come as something of a new revelation to policy makers! What matters now is that this insight translates into clear and rigorous thinking about the processes of learning and their application across education. It also has implications for how we shape other institutions that provide for young people, and it gives us ideas for reframing their practices.

In the chapter 'Types of Secure Establishment in Children and Young People in Custody' (Maggie Blyth et al. 2009), I tried to show how ideas of attach-ment and nurturing principles may be used to inform and support the deliv-ery of more effective regimes for young people placed in secure accommoda-tion. These ideas were expounded more fully in my book Working with Young People in Secure Accommodation – From Chaos to Culture (Rose, 2002). Both the chapter and book start from the point of having a clear view about the processes of child development; an understanding of the vital signifi-cance of relationships in promoting healthy emotional development; knowl-edge about the sequential schema of brain development; and, in particular, recognition of the importance of adolescence as a window of opportunity for influencing and changing behaviour. With these starting points as the basis of thinking, it becomes possible to conceptualise and design a regime that will radically change the way in which secure establishments operate and improve dramatically their effectiveness in preparing young people for life in the outside community.

But the point is not just about improving the performance and quality of work in secure accommodation. One of the current debates in youth justice is about the relationship between youth justice services and other services for children in the local authority. Beyond issues of budgets and who pays for what, there is a more fundamental question to be answered: how do we think about our children and young people, irrespective of whether or not their behaviour puts them into the orbit of the police and the court system? If, at the level of policy formation, we were able to think about children from a de-velopmental perspective, and if were able to recognise and resource activities and programmes aimed at sustaining healthy growth and development, then a wholly different environment for practice would be created. Such a change in the practice environment, however, would need to be accompanied by a considerable investment and re-focusing of training courses for students and workers to enable them to take advantage of the revised policy framework. The question we need to ask, as Marjorie Boxall put it, is not what has gone wrong with this child, but what has not gone right and what can be done to remedy that?

• The classroom offers a safe base

In a nurture group, the organisation of the environment and the way the group is managed helps to contain the children's anxiety. The nurture group room offers a balance of educational and domestic experiences aimed at supporting the development of the children's relationship with each other and with the staff. A kitchen area and dining table, soft seating and furnishings are set alongside tables for more formal 'academic' work. The room provides opportunities for children to play, to dress up and to explore.

The nurture group is organised around a structured day with predictable routines, with great attention paid to detail by adults who are reliable and consistent in their approach to the children. It is gratifying to note of recent instances where the design of a new school building has included a nurture group room in the overall provision. Many of the features of the nurture room, however, are also important in the design and furnishing of general classroom space, whilst some teachers of young children would claim that they are indispensable features of all good settings for this age group.

However, whilst the specific issues of physical design clearly relate to in-school provision, there are lessons to be learned about the quality and design of all spaces and accommodation in which work with children, families and young people is carried out. In addition, it is important to think behind the 'physical' characteristics and to remind ourselves of the underlying ideas that shape this particular principle. The phrase 'a safe base' immediately takes us back into attachment theory and the relationship between infant and mother. It is within this relationship that infants begin their exploration of the world as they test out boundaries to find out what is safe and what is not, confident in having the safe base of the mother to whom they can return when things become too difficult or frightening. The establishment of this 'safe base' is the foundation for all later learning experiences and plays an important part in the nature and quality of a child's longer term pattern in forming and sustaining relationships.

Working with abuse and neglect

In work with abused or neglected children, the importance of attachment has been increasingly recognised, with some researchers suggesting that 80% of maltreated children display insecure attachment reactions and behaviours (Howe et al. 1999). Having a clear understanding of the implications for a child's development in situations where, for whatever reason, the attachment relationship may be impaired is crucial. Similarly, it is essential to develop the observational skills required to identify situations where neglect or abuse may be occurring, and to develop the ability to interpret the worrying, insecure attachment behaviours that may be clues to what is happening to a child in their wider network. This requires considerable skill and experience not just in relation to knowing about infants and children, but also in relating to the adults involved. Although in a particular instance these adults may be perpetrators, research indicates the likelihood that in the past they may also have been victims of abuse. Developing this knowledge and skills base needs to be a key element in training programmes for all social work staff and in allied professional fields where individuals have the responsibility for identifying, investigating or treating families with children and young people who are suffering neglect or abuse or who may have witnessed extreme violence.

Planning for permanency and continuity

There are also implications in all of this for the way in which child-care services are organised to support what can be very difficult case work or treatment decisions. The emphasis placed on permanency planning for children in the public care system is commendable and it picks up on critical aspects of establishing and maintaining a child's 'safe base' upon which they can continue to develop and grow healthily. Achieving stability and continuity in a child's experience is essential if damage caused by early disruption to the attachment relationship is to be minimised and eventually healed.

It is, however, important to support and where possible to strengthen existing attachment relationships, whether with biological parents, relatives, friends or siblings. This is the focus of preventative work, trying to engage with the child in their family. However, this may not always be possible, at least for a period of time. If a child does have to be removed from their home, it is essential that this is done sensitively and in the context of an understanding of what it means for the child in terms of their existing relationships. It must also be done with the intention of providing settled and continuing relationships in the future. We shall think more about this in the section on transitions; for now our focus is on the importance of maintaining continuity for children who may have to experience changes of placement, including removal from their family and home.

It is interesting to ask, who does provide the essential continuity for such children? In my work as the professional advisor to HM Prison Service, it was my role to attend case conferences on young people aged between 10 and 17 years old who had been sentenced to long-term custody for 'grave crimes'. This entailed visiting every secure facility in England and Wales where these young people (around 500 at any one time) were being looked after. There is surprisingly little research about this group (Boswell 1995), but one of the distinguishing characteristics is the individuality of the circumstances of these young people and the way they present. This is what makes planning services or intervention strategies for the most vulnerable and challenging children and young people so difficult. However, there are a number of factors that can be clustered together to help think about these young people and what experiences may have contributed to their current situation. Michael Rutter and colleagues identify a number of key points:

- Early onset of antisocial behaviour associated with Attention Deficit Hyperactivity Disorder

- The age of onset, i.e. early or adolescent-specific

- Association with violence

- Psychopathy

- Mental Disorder (linked to learning disability and substance abuse.)

(Rutter et al. 1998: 96–111)

Roger Bullock, Michael Little and Spencer Millham from the Dartington Research Unit in Secure Treatment Outcomes (1998) track the 'careers' of those young people whose pathway through the care system eventually leads them to a placement in secure accommodation.

According to the Dartington study the careers of these most difficult young people may be tracked along one of the following paths: experience of long term state care or special education; a very serious one off offence; serious and persistent offending or in the phenomenon of the 'adolescent erupter', i.e. those young people who only come to the attention of agencies in early or mid adolescence and then pass rapidly through the system into secure accommodation.

(Rose 2002: 27)

They also confirm that the characteristics of these groups of young people are not uniform:

The young people in secure treatment centres are clearly a very heterogeneous group. Although they meet the criteria for placement in terms of disorder and danger in all other aspects they are very varied...As a

group they display a higher than expected rate for almost every disad-
vantage and behavioural difficulty. However, no single characteristic
dominates the population.

(Bullock et al. 1998: 46)

Gwyneth Boswell (1995) noted the extraordinarily high levels of loss and be-
reavement in the course of the relatively short life spans of young people who
had been sentenced to long-term custody. In the case review meetings I attended with young people in custody, two features became apparent: one was
the fact that many of these young people were known about by a whole raft
of services and agencies, and more importantly had been known by them for
a number of years; and second, there was a marked absence from their lives
of a single, continuous adult presence or relationship. Multiple placements,
changes of social workers and involvement by one agency after another (usually for a further assessment) had contributed to a lack of stability and continuity in these young people's relationships. These factors provide at least
part of the answer to our original question about who provides continuity
for these children and young people; the answer being, very often, no-one!

The importance of establishing and maintaining a 'safe base' for the most vulnerable of children and young people has to translate into case-work decision
making and planning, and be supported by the organisations and systems
within which this work occurs. To have any real meaning 'Permanency Planning' must prioritise the provision of settings for children and young people
to do the following: promote their continuing experience within a network of
relationships; establish and develop individual identity; provide them with a
sense of belonging (through safe, stable living environments); and guarantee
ongoing, accepting and unconditional emotional connections with all those
entrusted with their care and well-being.

• **Nurture is essential for the development of self-esteem**

> *Nurture involves listening and responding. In a nurture group 'eve-*
> *rything is verbalised' with an emphasis on the adults engaging with*
> *the children in reciprocal shared activities e.g. play / meals / reading*
> */talking about events and feelings. Children respond to being valued*
> *and thought about as individuals, so in practice this involves notic-*
> *ing and praising small achievements; 'nothing is hurried in nurture*
> *groups.*

(NGN website, *'about nurture groups'*)

The description of how this principle works out in the daily life of a nurture group captures the mood that nurture group staff are trying to create through their approach to the children in the group. A child's development of a positive and balanced view of their self-worth and of their place in the world around them, hopefully with confident expectations that this world is likely to act kindly towards them, is largely dependent on the quality of their attachment relationships and their interactions with primary care figures. It is these relationships, together with the subsequent experiences that follow, which contribute to the acquisition of another vital ingredient for a child's healthy growth; namely, resilience.

Whilst there is a clear link between attachment and resilience, it is also clear that the capacity to withstand adversity in life's circumstances is also dependent on possessing, at sufficiently useful levels, an ability to solve problems, to think positively, and to be able to use friendships and relationships for support and guidance. Developing resilience in those children who have experienced very difficult early circumstances needs to be at the heart of all direct work done with them, preferably set in the context of stable and continuous relationships. Writing in the Guardian (2006), Sir Al Aynsley Green, who was at that time the Children's Commissioner for England, commented:

> *Children who show persistent behavioural difficulties are often very troubled, with longstanding anxieties that relate to poor attachment and bonding in infancy.... we need to look at new approaches to promoting resilience.'*

> (*The Guardian*, 19 January 2006)

This is a key task in the foster care setting where the placement secures the essential stable environment, and the consistent daily routines provided by the foster carers become the context of shared activities that, over time, give children an enhanced sense of their own self-worth and a greater ability to achieve success in life.

Of course, that is the ideal. To achieve this requires the support of a whole system in which planning is paramount, resources are focused on the main task, and the system itself thinks about and prioritises the needs of children, rather than seeing the goal of a placement as being a fulfilment of quotas or the achievement of a target number.

Whilst it is undoubtedly through experiencing stable and secure relationships in a reliable and predictable environment that a child's resilience is increased, there are also specific activities that can support this. In the same way as structured programmes and activities help to develop a child's emotional awareness, so they can support the development of resilience. Similarly, however, it is the context in which such programmes are delivered, including the quality of the relationship that a child has with the adults delivering them, that makes the significant difference.

Schools have a vital role to play in such programmes and this is part of the value of SEAL, for example. In a study carried out between 1990 and 1995, the late Dr. Edith Grotberg (who was at the time a senior research scientist at the Civitan International Research Centre at the University of Alabama, Birmingham), looked at how parents and caretakers handled a variety of challenges, such as earthquakes, fires, floods, war, poverty, illness, death in the family, loss of income, or a major move. Her findings offer insight into how best to teach resiliency to different children at different ages. A number of key points emerged from her research:

- Children can learn how to be more resilient, regardless of their IQ.

- Children learn resilience from their parents up to the age of 11; after that, they learn from their peers.

- Parents and caregivers find it easy to teach resilience when a child is young, vulnerable, and helpless; yet they find it difficult when dealing with rebellious kids.

- Affluence doesn't seem to matter. Parents in developing nations teach resilience as often as those in affluent countries.

Punishment and blame are counterproductive, Grotberg says. 'It's not about putting guards with guns in schools. We need to teach resilience and reach out to kids who are troubled and depressed.' (Grotberg 1995)

What stands out through the report are the significance of the early years, the centrality of family experiences in building resilience, and the importance of creating a supportive and non-judgmental environment in which adults, children and young people are enabled to work collaboratively.

• Language is a vital means of communication

It is, perhaps, one of the unsurprising findings in the research literature of nurture groups that in the groups there are many more inter-personal interactions of a verbal kind between adults and children, and between children and children, than is the case in a normal classroom setting. The comparatively small size of the group obviously is a factor in this, but the underlying reason is much more to do with the emphasis placed on encouraging verbal exchanges and the focused work to improve children's language skills. In both the formal and informal aspects of a group, opportunities are created for children to talk to each other and to the adults, to listen to others, and to begin to develop the vital skill of empathy. The 'breakfast' routine is a good example of how social learning can be linked to 'curriculum' work and underpinned by the creation of situations in which children are helped to communicate a range of feelings and emotions through using language.

> *The daily ritual of breakfast is acted out in hundreds of nurture groups across the United Kingdom every school day. The two adults, usually a teacher and a learning support assistant who run the group use the opportunity of eating together to practise good social behaviours but more importantly to encourage the children to talk, to listen to others and to experience a sense of being valued and 'thought about' by significant adult figures.*

(Rose 2004)

In all settings with children, the use of language and the development of the skills of children and young people to express themselves through verbal communication is a priority. Of course, we need to understand the importance and meaning of non-verbal communications from children and young people, and also the value of other expressive means of communicating feelings (through music or art for example). However, it is surely the aim of all therapeutic endeavours to stop or prevent acting-out behaviours, and to encourage a process of thinking and talking about problems.

A foster carer in a support group recounted how she had struggled to communicate with one of the children in her care. Alex, who had been diagnosed with extreme autism, attended his nursery on a daily basis; but there, the emphasis was on using sign language to communicate and the carer was told not to try to keep talking with him. Intuitively, and with help from a very supportive worker from the local CAMHS team, she persisted with using verbal language, and over time she saw Alex begin to respond and start trying to use words to express his needs and feelings. Part of the explanation for this difference in approach may be something to do with pressures on staff time and the way in which, in such circumstances, short-term management strategies become preferred to the demands of longer-term patient and persistent care. However, it also significant to note that it was a foster carer who, largely intuitively and through her relationship with the child, struggled on with developing his speech and extending his use of language.

How language is used by adults in communicating with children and young people is also of real significance. Perhaps the most striking example of this is in young offender institutions where the ways in which prison officers talk to (and about) the young people in their charge is a real indicator of an establishment's culture and its general approach to the tasks of care. However, the same principle applies whatever the setting may be. There is a wider relevance here in regard to the use of language to which we have already referred; namely, the disconnectedness between the nature of professional language and its terminology and ordinary speech used in daily intercourse. There is also a gap between the way in which current formats for recording case review meetings or case-work visits are structured, and what is required for capturing the free, flowing nature of the narratives they are seeking to reflect. We shall return to this problem in chapter 6.

• **All Behaviour is communication**

This principle underlies appropriate adult responses to children's often challenging or difficult behaviour. The question to be posed in such situations is, 'Given what I know about this child and their development, what are they trying to tell me?' Thinking about what a child may be communicating through their behaviour helps adults to respond in firm but non-punitive ways, and without being provoked to anger or despair. If a child senses their feelings are being understood, this helps to diffuse a difficult or potentially violent situation. It is the adult, acting on behalf of the child, who provides the essential containment and makes the link between the child's experiences of the external world with the turmoil of their feelings in their inner world.

This kind of thinking is the basis of all good therapeutic work with children and young people, irrespective of the setting in which it occurs. Behaviour is not regarded as an entity in its own right but as a communication from the child about their chaotic, internal state.

Finding ways to respond to and deal with antisocial behaviour in society, specifically amongst young people, has been a main plank of government policy over recent years. The introduction and use of Antisocial Behaviour Orders within the youth justice system has stimulated a wide-ranging debate, not just about their effectiveness, but of the consequences their introduction appears to have had in furthering the criminalisation of children and young people and in increasing the numbers of young people in custody. Similarly, the issue of behaviour in schools has been at the forefront of a number of initiatives under a 'Behaviour and Attendance' agenda, which has yielded specific intervention strategies and the creation of new, professional roles such as Behaviour Support Teachers who work in designated teams in schools.

The links between antisocial behaviour and early attachment experiences are increasingly well documented. So too is recognition of the effectiveness of interventions which, like nurture groups, build their practice on this knowledge base. This is illustrated in the reports commissioned by the government from Sir Alan Steer (Steer Report 2009).

The influential report from the international charity WAVE Trust, '*Violence and what to do about it*' (The WAVE report 2005), reiterates the significance of understanding the complexities of child development, including the way that the infant brain grows, as the key to later strategies for intervening in situations of domestic and other forms of violence. 'The single most effective way to stop producing people with the propensity to violence is to ensure infants are reared in an environment that fosters their development of empathy. The surest way to achieve this is by supporting parents in their developing attunement with their infants' (The WAVE report, 2005: point 8 Executive Summary).

It is enormously encouraging when prestigious reports and published research consistently reaffirm the importance of early and preventative intervention, setting out clearly the conditions within which children are able to thrive and in effect supporting the argument that by taking these ideas seriously, it is possible to devise intervention strategies that make a real difference. The challenge, once again, is to create policy and organisational contexts that properly resource and support these approaches.

• Transitions are important in children's lives

The sixth and final principle drawn from the nurture group model could be described as one that completes the circle, i.e. thinking about transitions takes us back to ideas about the importance of developmental processes. The notion of transition conveys the idea of changing from one condition to another – a process that is important for all children, but especially for those who are vulnerable and damaged.

Originally, being part of a nurture group helped a child to make the difficult transition from home to school. Nowadays, with their use across all age ranges and stages, this particular transition is not the exclusive focus for nurture groups. Another major transition for children is the move from primary to secondary school, and there are a number of instances where nurture groups have successfully helped children to negotiate the changes involved in this process.

Whilst these examples are based on nurture groups in schools, there are many other settings in which the management of transitions is critical. On a daily basis, children are required to make a number of transitions. In school, they move frequently between classes and different adults, and many children make daily transitions from home to childminder, to school, to yet another childminder after school, and then back to home. Changes in routine are invariably difficult for vulnerable children and require careful management with preparation and support.

It is well recognised that for young people admitted to any form of secure accommodation, the first night, spent alone in a locked room or cell, presents a potentially high risk for self-harm. This is the case not only for young people who may have a history of self-harming behaviour, but for a good number of others as well who find the sense of isolation simply overwhelming and frightening. All establishments pay particular attention to this aspect of their regime, whilst some have developed special 'first night' procedures and have identified certain items that young people may wish to have in their cells to help keep them calm and reassured about their safety, e.g. reading materials, a radio, and paper and pens for writing or drawing.

Similarly, it is known that for young people leaving their secure unit or being released from custody, the first night of freedom presents a variety of risks. These include over enthusiastic celebrations or a reintroduction to an antisocial peer group, both of which may result in further offending. It may be, however, that as is the case for far too many young people, no preparation has been made for their leaving; there is no identified place to stay and, more importantly, there is no-one around to meet the young person and to help them settle into their new accommodation. In the experience of custody, the sense of isolation can be as sharp on the outside as it is on the inside for some young people.

In foster care, similar issues arise with the processes of how children and young people arrive and depart from their placement. Being brought to somewhere strange, by someone you perhaps don't know very well to stay with people you haven't met before, with little idea as to why you are there, would be enough to disturb most adults, let alone anxious, worried children!

Moving on from a settled foster care home to a new placement can be just as worrying and frightening. This is why it is so important that an understanding of these feelings and of what the process means to children and young people should feature as the main point of decision making in case reviews or in social work offices. Friday afternoon changes of placement and responding to a crisis just before the weekend are still an all-too-frequent scenario in social work offices and foster homes.

Inevitably, there are reasons why children and young people need to move on – and whether the decision is for the child to go home or to other carers, not all of these are negative. The planning for such changes, however, must consider how to preserve a sense of continuity for the child, and positive attachment relationships with existing carers should not simply discontinue just because a child returns home or moves onto another placement.

Developing attachments and establishing relationships need to be goals when planning for both short-term and long-term placements; it is through developing positive attachments and creating a nurturing and responsive care environment that foster carers help children cope with change and move on to new situations.

The same challenge presents itself with this principle as with the others: how can this thinking and understanding translate into policy directives and be supported through organisational management and practices?

WHAT THIS MEANS FOR ORGANISATIONS

The ideas that I have put forward are critical for the development of more effective and safer practices. As a basis for all healthy human growth and development, there is an irrefutable argument for their centrality in the education and training programmes of all workers with children, young people and their families. However, there is still the issue of the conflict of agendas to be resolved. The reasonable requirement to measure organisational performance has to be balanced with delivering services that meet the real needs of children and young people; these must include practices that embody nurturing approaches and address the fundamental challenges of providing secure attachments and building resilience through relational experiences.

For organisations to provide their front line staff with the security and containment they need (and which are essential for meeting the needs of the most vulnerable and damaged children, young people and families), they have to be enabled to develop cultures that reflect and enshrine these priorities. To work thoughtfully and safely, people require structures that provide them with a protected space for thinking and reflection. To be effective, professional supervision must be regular and challenging, whilst staff meetings and training have to happen as planned, despite all the other pressures that beset institutions and organisations. Workers, too, have to accept their responsibilities and must ensure that they play their part in facilitating the regular occurrence of these essential activities.

To achieve the above requires structural issues to be meaningfully addressed, such as workload allocation and the recruitment and retention of front line workers, especially social workers and foster carers. It also means devising systems that recognise the importance of maintaining continuity in key workers over years – not months or weeks, as is currently all too often the case. The systems must also incorporate a policy framework that is committed to nurturing practice and supportive of its development with proper resourcing. It is a mindset issue!

ORGANISATIONS AS CONTAINERS OF THINKING

In order for therapeutic work to be safe and effective, organisations also have to be 'containers of thinking' with appropriate structures and management to allow this to happen. In the same way that we would talk about the importance of adults 'holding in mind' the children and young people with whom they are working, so too must adult workers feel that their organisation – and in particular their managers – are 'holding them in mind' and providing a 'safe base' or organisational context for their work. Those who are responsible for the creation of the policy framework, and those who manage services, need to be aware of the realities of what it means to work with and to look after children and young people who have experienced high levels of neglect and abuse. Although they may not be directly involved in practice on a daily basis, they have to be prepared to respond to the kind of reactions that this work generates. Senior managers in particular have to be able to recognise and respond to the reactions of their frontline workforce, but also to those of the wider public who will have very strong and often ambivalent feelings about the nature of the task.

There is a continuum along which organisations may be placed that marks their responses to the task of containment and shows how the culture of the organisation is reacting to the challenge. In a number of recent high-profile events and subsequent enquiries, there are examples of organisations and services that have received criticism for operating at both ends of this continuum.

At one end are the organisations whose emphasis and priority are the achievement of compliance, and for whom this is the main organisational goal. In these organisations, there is an over use of regulation to prescribe practice, and the emphasis on output, routine and structure are ends in themselves, rather than providing boundaries within which relationships are fostered and allowed to develop. These services or organisations are reflective of current policy and central government demands for performance measurement, and they are prone to the sorts of failure we have identified earlier.

At the other end are the organisations and services that are best described as being overwhelmed by chaos. These organisations are routinely characterised by high levels of staff absence and sickness, unfilled vacancies, poor recruitment practices and low staff morale and retention rates. In practice, staff are often late for meetings, and appointments are frequently cancelled or missed.

Performance at either end of the continuum would be likely to produce serious consequences and certainly not provide the kind of setting or context required for safe practice with people whose lives are already chaotic or whose behaviour may be dangerous. Although written specifically about secure units, the following quote has application to wider organisational practice where the task is that of bringing stability to chaotic and distressed people in adverse circumstances:

> *Making a transition from chaos to culture is not achieved by the rigid imposition of rules and regulations, hoping that if only we could have more control over people or events then chaos would be eliminated. It is achieved through struggling to make space for thinking so that informed decisions can be made, even if only about what to do next.*

(Rose 2002)

Professor Robert Hinshelwood reminds us of the dangers of allowing chaos to reign in organisations struggling to care for vulnerable and chaotic people:

> *Poorly organised institutions will risk enhancing the internal disorganisation of their severely disordered members, who in turn will tend to dismantle and disturb the organisation of the institution.*

(Hinshelwood 1999)

'CLEAR THINKING ABOUT MIXED EMOTIONS'

'Clear thinking about mixed emotions' is how W. H. Auden once described great art, and it is an apt description of what needs to be achieved by organisations whose task involves working with chaotic or abusive families. A thinking organisation has to maintain its ability to 'think under fire' or, to put it another way, it must remain stable and functioning in situations that generate huge amounts of anxiety and stress. Neither becoming procedurally rigid (through seeking compliance) nor succumbing to the chaos around (by allowing structures to fall apart) are satisfactory responses to the challenge of protecting vulnerable children and young people and of providing them with the right experiences for healthy growth and personal development. There are consequences for organisations unable to provide sufficient containment for its workforce, and there are serious implications for workers who are trying to engage – on a daily basis – with people who are at best resistant and, at worst, highly manipulative. It is to these that we now turn.

Chapter 5

What do you do when there is nothing you can do?

"I am afraid to think what I have done"
Shakespeare, Macbeth, Act II scene ii

In chapter 1, we saw how the overwhelming nature of some experiences renders us unable to think clearly or rationally. It is a typical feature of many of the situations that face workers involved with very damaged or traumatised people; they feel a great sense of helplessness and hopelessness, not just about the circumstances of the children and families they are wanting to help, but in their own ability to make a difference.

Such feelings are often expressions of despair, although they may sound very plausible and rational: "Look at the level of deprivation and poverty on this estate. How am I possibly going to be able to make any difference to this family?" So says the over-burdened social worker, hurrying from one appointment to the next, a quota of visits to complete before the end of the day. "What difference can I make in my classroom? I haven't the time; and in any case, when they go home at night, they just forget it all and the family's influence is so much greater." So says the teacher, with records to complete and reports to write. "They're only here for a short while. I'll do the best I can, but they are likely to move before any real good can be done." So says the foster carer, irritated at being kept in the dark about the plans for the child for whom they are providing a home, and resigned to just being asked to 'warehouse' them until the next planning meeting takes place.

These are generalised feelings arising from the sheer magnitude of the task that these workers are expected to do – or at least, this is how it appears to them. However, the strength of the feeling which accompanies the thought 'There is nothing I can do, but I am expected to do something' is greatly magnified by the specific circumstances of a child or by the particular situation in which the adult and child are in some sort of confrontation or crisis together.

Whilst many workers accept that achieving even small steps towards change is difficult and frustrating, they also realise that this is 'part of the job' and are prepared to accept inevitable disappointment. What heightens irritation in our current climate, however, are the demands and unrealistic expectations placed on front line staff. For social-care staff, this may be the demand to achieve targets for certain measurable changes in short and defined time periods. For teachers, it is the expectation that children reach unrealistic and arbitrary levels of attainment based chronological age rather than developmental stage.

In more complex cases, where there is a need for sensitive intervention over longer periods of time, these pressures are compounded by the very nature of the work itself. The unravelling of a family dynamic where there may be hidden abuse of children is not only intellectually challenging but often demands physical bravery to venture into a hostile or violent home situation. Such circumstances are certainly emotionally demanding. As we have already argued, this kind of work requires not only a skilled and experienced workforce, but an organisational context that is understanding and supportive.

DEFENDING AGAINST ANXIETY

Those directly involved in abusive or neglectful situations will, over extended periods of time, build up patterns of behaviour and responses that serve to protect them from experiencing too painfully the horrors caused either by their own actions or by those around them. In the same way, so too workers and their organisations may develop defensive mechanisms to protect against the anxiety and distress that working in such situations generates. Recognising the nature of these defences, and understanding how they influence behaviour and responses, is part of the task for an individual worker and for their supervisor. Their joint thinking contributes to what becomes a shared narrative between all those involved in the circumstances of those children, young people and families about whom there are serious concerns.

There are a number of different ways to think about the meaning and the processes of the psychological defences to which we have alluded. It is not within the remit of this book to discuss their detailed functions, and further reading is suggested. However, the main processes that will be immediately recognisable include denial, projection and splitting – all of which can be very powerful in frustrating the capacity of a worker or teams of workers to think about the situations they engage in.

From the perspective of the client, one of the main purposes of their defensive behaviour is to prevent the essential thinking required by the professionals, which will lead them to deeper understanding and appropriate interventions. Of course, a client may be unaware of the effects of their behaviour and may become extremely resistant to the attempts of the worker to confront it. The worker's task is to recognise the nature of the defence and to seek ways of overcoming the resistance. A frequent recurring difficulty is that the worker, through their relationship with the client, is an active participant in the process and, as a result of their own experiences, may be susceptible to collusion and avoidance. This is the tricky nature of projection, as Professor Robert Young points out; projections find a willing, if unsuspecting, target.

> *When we project into another it is rather like fly-fishing: we cast something out that teases something out; it catches something there and brings it out. What we catch may have been swimming about minding its own business until our attention is caught by its lure ... the projection finds its Other and evokes (and usually exaggerates) something that was there but perhaps not virulently so.*

(Robert Young 1995)

Children and young people who live in very stressful situations, or who have experienced trauma or witnessed domestic violence over long periods of time, often have a strong sense of their own hopelessness and helplessness. This exacerbates their already ingrained feelings of low self-worth. These children and young people are very difficult to communicate with; their trauma renders them almost speechless. They are without the words to convey the deep distress and pain that they feel. In such circumstances, the child may opt for actions rather than words. As these may be antisocial or aggressive, it is not uncommon to hear people make comments such as, "They act first and think afterwards." The problem is, of course, that these traumatised children are not able to think afterwards either!

These are complex processes; we are not just talking about bad behaviour but exploring various well developed and entrenched defence mechanisms employed to prevent exposure or, in the case of a child, to resist 'penetration' by adults – literally, in some cases. The consequences of what life would be like without these defences may be horrific for a young child, and too horrendous even to think about.

In Shakespeare's tragedy, Macbeth confronts the terrible crime that he has committed, namely the murder of a King. It is the horror of his action that leads him to cry out, 'I am afraid to think what I have done'. Overwhelmed by the tormenting memories that come to him in delusions of ghosts and daggers, the past comes flooding into his mind. This is the stuff of nightmares or, as Macbeth so dramatically expresses it, the 'murder of sleep'. For those who work in residential or foster-care settings, dealing with the effects of these 'nightmares' may be more immediate, resulting in many disturbed or sleepless nights.

The re-emergence of feelings that are so traumatic they defy rational thought seems to be particularly acute at night-time or first thing in the morning. They are often triggered by what seem inconsequential actions on the part of other people, or even by other sensory experiences such as smell or taste. This is why bed times, morning routines, eating, washing, or using the bathroom can be so difficult for many children. The sensitivities of residential staff or foster carers have to be finely tuned to the needs of the children in their care, and these key routines must be carried out with fresh thought on a daily basis. We shall return to this later in the chapter.

TIME AND PLACE

When a traumatised child is in a rage, they will often scream at the adult who is there at that moment with an anger that seems utterly disproportionate to the circumstances, and with a personal vindictiveness that is hard to understand. Often in such moments, what we hear from the child is clearly coming from some other time and place. Much of the work undertaken in schools, by foster carers, or by residential workers is very much 'here and now'. The adults respond to the immediate distress as best they can by using information and material from the current situation to understand and calm the child. For the child in the midst of a tantrum, however, there is a genuine confusion between 'here and now' with 'now and then'.

As S. J. Lec (1965) puts it: 'The sequence of time is an illusion ... we fear most the past that returns.' For a distressed child, that returning past is their reality. T.S. Eliot (1968) put it another way:

> Time present and time past
> Are both perhaps present in time future,
> And time future contained in time past.

In the context of work with children and young people, this phenomenon is often present when a child or young person makes an allegation against an adult carer. That is why dealing with allegations is always challenging and provokes high levels of anxiety. It is particularly puzzling when a child makes the allegation against a member of staff with whom previously they appear to have had a close relationship. Of course, the most straightforward answer to this dilemma is that the child is telling the truth, and the trust they have placed in an adult responsible for their care has been betrayed. However, experience suggests that this is certainly not always the case and something that requires more consideration is going on.

It is at this point that those investigating allegations and complaints need to be insightful, understanding that there is more 'content' in the relationships between children and professional adults who work closely with them than any checklist approach to child protection is likely to reveal. For children and young people who have suffered abuse or trauma over a period of time, the memories of that abuse do not remain in the past but become actions in the here and now. Such memories may be triggered by a number of things around them, including the experience of a close relationship; so at the point where they feel threatened by the emotional intimacy they are experiencing, they act out for their own defence and survival.

We have already considered the importance of secure attachment for healthy development and how the quality of that secure attachment helps to build up the resilience needed to withstand and overcome adverse events and circumstances later in life. Knowing about a child's early attachment experience helps to provide links between the child's 'then' and the shared 'now,' aiding understanding about the reasons for current reactions and behaviour.

Of course, there is not always a straightforward causal or linear relationship between past and present, but thinking about these issues can help in situations that are often very difficult to tolerate or that threaten to become overwhelming. The following quote refers to staff who work in secure accommodation, but it could equally apply to any setting where adults work closely with children and young people:

> *The ideas of Attachment Theory provide an interesting way to reflect upon the meaning of current presenting behaviour from young people. Such reflection may also provide important clues not just about why a young person is behaving in a particular way but why certain approaches that might be used to establish a relationship are more or less successful. Staff are often puzzled as to why some young people do not appear to respond to their well intentioned and genuinely offered approaches of support. In fact the experience is often one of strong rejection which can be dispiriting and puzzling to new staff who cannot understand why their best efforts seem to be thrown back in their face by the young people they are trying to help. Being able to depersonalise this rejection and to see it in the context of how a young person may themselves have been consistently rejected or never had an opportunity to make a good or lasting relationship is an important learning point.*

(Rose 2002: 53)

HOLDING ON AND BEING THERE

A recurring assumption throughout this book is the importance of relationships as the basis for effective intervention. Today, so much emphasis is placed on 'activity' as the primary concern for intervention: in school, this is the preoccupation with curriculum; in youth justice, it is the reliance on programmes; in much of social work, it is the completion of questionnaires, checklists and information collation through the filling-in of forms or inputting data into electronic systems.

Although it is obviously beneficial for adults and children to share in worthwhile activities, these are, at best, a vehicle through which relationships may begin and subsequently grow. It is often the case that the really powerful therapeutic activities are the most obvious and ordinary. In residential or fostering work, it is the routine activities of daily living that provide the richest opportunities for meaningful engagement and conversation, and for sharing and learning in the context of a nurturing relationship. In schools, it is those exchanges that occur outside of formal lessons that matter, what Fritz Redl (1966) called 'the in-between times' – the comment made in passing, the shared personal reflection, the remark that shows that an adult has remembered something important for the child, even the look that shows appreciation or reassurance. Such 'in-between times' all too often go unnoticed by the adult, but are remembered forever by the child.

Of course, this kind of thinking and understanding has to be built into the life of the work place, whether a school, social-work team, residential unit or foster home. They also have to be sustained in the face of a child's behaviour, which, as we have described, may appear bewildering or even frightening for adults. But it is precisely at these moments that the adults have to hold on to the thinking that is required to make sense of the behaviour and to plan for the future.

For as we have seen, many of the actions of a child or young person are intended to prevent thinking – certainly their own, for that is beyond them at the time, but also to prevent the thinking of the adults as well. The fact remains, however, that if the children and young people cannot think, then it is something the adult group has to do on their behalf, at least initially. All workers have to develop that capacity to 'think under fire', to keep going and to keep thinking in the face of all adversity.

THE QUESTION ANSWERED?

It is here that we begin to glimpse an answer to the question posed at the beginning of this chapter: 'What do you do when there is nothing you can do?' Well, you can think, you can stay with the placement; you can keep visiting the child in the family home; or you can hold the child or the family 'in mind', waiting for the moment when – through the painstaking task of building a relationship – you detect even the smallest insight or step forward.

To sustain such an approach, however, requires humility and the patience to work at the client's pace. It demands time for relationships to develop, and for a continuity of presence that can only be achieved by the same worker being available and ready to respond over an extended period of time, as well as being there to ensure regular and ongoing contact.

These are principles that apply to all work settings and if we accept their importance, then there are major implications for how policy is formulated and for management practices. We already know that stability and continuity are essential for the healthy growth of an infant, that the basis for all early learning is relational, and that healthy physical growth is linked inextricably to receiving emotional nourishment; so we should not be too surprised to realise that the same principles apply to organisational structures, which need to be nourished within a policy framework that shows understanding of what is required for effective implementation and delivery of services.

It is beyond individual staff to maintain this approach, however. This is the reason the core values and structures of the systems and organisations have to be compatible with the requirements of individual case-work and therapy. If effective nurturing practices in all of our institutions – including the secure estate and across the full range of our services for children and young people – are to be truly valued and acknowledged, then the wider framework for policy formulation and management implementation has to be shaped. This needs to be formed in ways that promote and support the nurture of these most vulnerable children, young people and families.

THE WAY THINGS ARE NOW

Sadly, many of our current institutions and services do not reflect the core principles of nurture, largely because they do not sit within policy and wider management frameworks that genuinely embrace these ideas.

In a recent report (October 2009), Birmingham's Children's Services were strongly criticised and described as 'not fit for purpose' in a number of important areas. The report followed on from a series of reported child deaths within the authority over the past four years. Amongst the issues raised were the following: the lack of senior managers in post; the failure to provide a strong management lead; the lack of experienced or senior staff to supervise a large and generally inexperienced workforce, who were left with the responsibility for initial assessments; inadequate case-file management; and the very poor state of repair of much of the residential accommodation for children and young people. Whilst the report acknowledged that many of the challenges faced by Birmingham are not unique to that authority and indeed are national challenges, e.g. the recruitment and retention of social workers, it was clear that the situation was disastrously unacceptable.

In a follow-up television interview, two of Birmingham's social workers were filmed visiting clients on an estate. The workers talked about the visits they were about to make and described how time for such visits was limited, and how the number of visits they were required to make had to be the focus of their attention, although they made clear that this situation was unsatisfactory and not of their choice. They were clearly aware of the need to take more time to understand certain family situations, rather than having to work with some arbitrary notion of how long a visit should take. In a comment, the Director of Children's Services indicated that one of the problems facing him and his staff was the enormous bureaucracy they had to contend with on a daily basis, filling in copious forms and completing other paper work demands.

Concerns over these issues are not readily allayed by another feature of current organisational life; namely, the constant re-organising and re-structuring of local authority departments. A climate in which people are uncertain about their jobs or are expected to re-apply for a post to which they had already been appointed breeds an uncertainty and instability that contra-indicates – to an alarming degree – the stability and continuity needed in the placement and care of the most vulnerable of children, young people and families. Maintaining organisational stability is an important factor and has to be addressed, not only structurally in terms of staff recruitment, but also through developing a real understanding of the deep significance it has for children, especially in terms of maintaining continuity in key relationships and in the time it takes for trust to develop.

A further aspect of the present work environment across services for children and families, which to some extent comes from trying to resolve the issues of time pressure and lack of resources, is the focus on short-term intervention strategies, which also serve to demonstrate achievement of outputs and outcomes. In a target driven, results-orientated culture, there is great pressure on frontline workers not only to fulfil their quota of visits, but to demonstrate their effectiveness in measurable terms. Taking the time to think, stay with a situation, or just to reflect and say that at that moment it is not clear what is happening doesn't cut the mustard for the purposes of audit.

One of the consequences of this is that workers in all settings are expected to find solutions within arbitrary timescales; being a professional carries high expectations of knowledge and expertise, so they are forced to put on a 'mask of competency' and show how they are on top of things by completing a checklist, writing a pre-formatted report, or filling in a form that shows how many times a family has been visited. A further consequence of this is the erosion of confidence, particularly amongst younger workers, in their own professional judgment.

In one situation, a young social worker expressed a surprising degree of anxiety when faced with the prospect of attending a meeting, because they feared the other people might know more than they did. Rather than be able to go to the meeting and share information, they really thought that as the social worker, they should have the answers to all the issues likely to be raised. Afraid that the 'mask of competence' might be exposed, they were preparing excuses as to why they might not attend. Fortunately, a more experienced colleague was able to reassure them and support them in fulfilling their responsibilities.

Much of what has been written above may be understood in the light of prevailing organisational models that value above all else the evidencing of high levels of activity and outputs. Individual workers become so busy (and are bureaucratised to such a degree) that their 'busyness' functions as part of their defence against having to spend time thinking about, hearing, or discussing the unfolding narratives of the true distress and pain being experienced by many children, young people and families.

RISK AND FEAR

A great number of people working in social care and education, including – and perhaps especially – foster carers, feel themselves to be under intense scrutiny as they perform their duties and carry out their daily tasks. They are fearful of what may happen if they are accused of behaving inappropriately, and they believe that they will not be supported if a problem arises. Immediate suspension, followed by drawn out and protracted periods of investigation, is the lot of many foster carers who are subject to allegations, and similar procedures and processes apply to other professionals.

There is no doubt that one of the reasons for the abundance of paper work and recording systems that beset all work settings is a perceived need for 'covering your back,' as the prospect of litigation looms large in many areas of professional life – and for many parts of society as a whole.

Fearing complaints or investigations is not just something for individual workers at whatever organisational level they may be operating, but becomes part of the agenda for whole organisations and services as well. Detailed systems for monitoring performance are underpinned by an anxiety about being able to show the 'paper trail' if things go wrong! This fear is increased by the pressure put on agencies and local authorities to perform for the purposes of inspection and audit. Inspection protocols are still largely reflective of the requirement to show, in statistical form, that various targets have been met and outputs achieved.

As we noted in chapter 3, we are living in an increasingly risk averse society and the effects of this are regarded by a growing number of people as having a serious and detrimental effect on the experience of childhood for thousands of children, (Gill 2007). Just as serious, however, is the link between the general trend towards restricting any activity that involves risk for children (which previously would have been regarded as a normal and acceptable part of growing up), and the effects of the current anxiety and fear of 'being complained about'. Rather than encouraging a culture of inquiry, in which curiosity and a degree of acceptable risk taking is regarded as normal, we are veering towards a culture of enquiry, in which every action is likely to be subjected to scrutiny and a report filed!

APPROACHES TO RISK ASSESSMENT

Ronald Doctor (2004) is a psychiatrist involved in the assessment and treatment of violent patients, working with people who are severely mentally disturbed. The assessment and management of risk are, therefore, central to his practice in a highly specialist setting. He describes two approaches to risk assessment, the application of which may be relevant to other areas of practice in which some kind of assessment and judgment about the potential risk for harm must be made, either in the case of individuals (to themselves or to others) or a situation.

The first is the actuarial approach, which is based on the collection and collation of certain 'facts' including demographic information and the number of previous episodes of violence. These are given a weighting value according to a pre-determined formula, and a figure, which aims to give a predictive score as to likely future behaviour, is arrived at. Second, there is the psychodynamic or clinical approach, in which an individual's pathology is explored through their relationship with their 'therapist' and the detail of those interactions is used as the basis for decision making. He summarises his conclusions:

> *It has come to be recognized by a number of researchers ... that the*

> *actuarial model of risk assessment based on epidemiology has failed.*
> *The most reliable risk assessment remains based essentially at an in-*
> *dividual clinical level, and this requires a clear conceptual framework*
> *in order to contain potentially dangerous and unpredictable acting*
> *out behaviour by the patient and severe anxiety in the workers.*

(Ronald Doctor, 2004: 52)

It is not the purpose of How Nurture Protects Children to argue the relative merits of these alternative approaches to assessing and managing risk.
Ronald Doctor is clear in his views, not only about the advantages of the
clinical over the actuarial approach in terms of making effective assessments
of risk, but of the associated difficulties with the clinical approach, especially
the demands it makes on the workers and its vital need to occur within a
'conceptual framework' that can contain the inevitable anxiety that arises in
the process.

EXAMPLES OF ASSESSING RISK

As director of a Secure Training Centre, I chaired a weekly meeting with
the purpose of assessing the level of risk presented by young people who
had been identified on admission as potentially at risk of self-harming, and
whose continuing 'training plan' needed to reflect any ongoing concerns. The
level at which the risk was assessed affected – at a practical level – the degree
of supervision required for the young person, particularly the frequency of
checks at night and also the nature of the furnishings and type of personal
items they were allowed to have in their room. In addition, however, the outcomes of the assessment greatly influenced the perceptions held by both the
staff and, of course, the other young people on the residential unit about that
individual.

As part of the meeting, we used information from previous placements and
whether or not the young person had attempted self-harm before, and we
referred to recorded observations of the young person in our centre, looking
at their behaviour in different settings. The focus of the discussion, however,
was to try to distil information from the staff who had worked directly with
the individual (on the units or in education) and knew him or her. We wanted
to find out what the staff's feelings were about the individual, what their relationship was, and what they thought in general. Taken all together, we made
decisions based on what was essentially the 'clinical' approach.

The other Secure Training Centre, managed by the same company and caring
for a similar group of young people, used a more rigid actuarial approach in

their assessment of risk. Data was collected and scored, with certain totals identified as representing degrees of risk and appropriate responses set out and implemented automatically.

I would argue that whilst there were no significant differences between the number of episodes of self-harm in the two centres (very low in both cases, given the histories of the young people being looked after), the clinical approach had a number of advantages: relationships became the focus of the work of the centre, improving the general ethos and atmosphere, and staff felt valued because their opinions mattered, and so their professional confidence grew exponentially.

Achieving this progress required the development of a supportive staff culture, the prioritisation of supervision and training, and clear statements about the practice model being implemented throughout the centre. In other words, the provision of the essential 'conceptual framework' urged by Ronald Doctor for containing the high levels of anxiety the work evokes. There was resistance from staff, who did indeed feel very anxious about the responsibility they felt they were being asked to assume, and they needed constant reassurance from the whole management team about both the collaborative nature of the work and how they would be supported if things were to go wrong.

CONFIDENT TO CARE

It is interesting to note how the particular discussion about risk assessment appears to mirror wider issues about the relative merits of different approaches to assessment and intervention, or indeed about the whole culture of practice in work with children, young people and families. The so-called actuarial approach reflects much of current practice in social care and education services. The emphasis on data collection – and the assumptions about the nature of evidence and what might be regarded as a depersonalising of the individual – separates the decision making about how to best meet a person's needs from any sense of having to establish a relationship over time, which would help gain an understanding of what those needs may be.

The clinical approach, whilst not rejecting the relevance of some of the data used for an actuarial approach to risk assessment, looks beyond this information, trusting in a relationship with the individual and using material gleaned from direct inter-personal work. This includes thinking and reflecting about feelings and using intuition to make sense of behaviours and plan future actions and interventions. In these circumstances, professional judgment counts and risk is contained by the development of a trusting relationship set in a supportive but challenging network of supervision and management oversight.

Whilst the above describes aspects of the current climate for professional practice, there are further considerations to be taken into account. The coming together of a number of other critical factors also has serious and detrimental implications for how children and young people are cared for. These are irrespective of whether the care is provided directly in foster homes or residential units, or how social workers and teachers use their time to address the needs of their vulnerable clients and pupils. There are the demands of bureaucracy, which means focus and energy are directed at the next report to be written, the next form to be completed, or the next meeting attended. There are the limitations of resources, with too few people to do the necessary sustained work – so appointments are cancelled and pressures of time restrict the amount of personal contact. There are the demands for quick solutions to problems so workers can 'sign off a piece of work' and move on to the next task. And there are the fears that arise from over regulation, as well as the anxiety and fantasy about what might happen if an allegation is made.

Taking all these factors together, workers whose practice brings them into direct contact with children, young people and families feel constrained and hampered. They believe their professional judgment is ignored or disregarded, feel generally unsupported in the work that they do, and think they will be blamed and punished if they make a mistake. Given the nature of the work, it may be that feeling unsupported, inadequate, incompetent, or left alone with the problem are inevitable consequences of the job (and best talked about within supervision, which should happen as part of the 'containing conceptual framework'). However, the policy and managerial context for current practice leads workers to seriously doubt their role and feel a lack of confidence when with children or young people in particular.

Many of the children and young people about whom we are thinking present with or portray an extreme vulnerability; much of this vulnerability stems from the insecure attachment experiences that are so characteristic of the populations of looked-after children and young people caught up in the youth justice system, especially those placed in some type of secure accommodation. However, there are still many children living with their families and going to school on a daily basis, who have similar profiles and present in similar ways, meaning that teachers and teaching assistants will also be confronted with this dilemma.

It is this vulnerability, projected by the children onto the adults who are caring for them, which powerfully contributes to the feelings of helplessness, inadequacy or isolation that the adults experience and which can be frankly disturbing. Understanding and coping with these projections requires adults who are confident in what they are doing and who have regular opportunities to think and talk about their work. Children and young people need adults who know them and are confident in their dealings with them. They need adults who can accept the projections, process them, and then pass them back to them in ways that they can understand and learn from. Children and young people need adults who can tolerate their behaviour but at the same time provide boundaries for their anxiety, and offer the nurturing that they may not have experienced before.

For children and young people to achieve healthy growth and development, it is essential that the principles from attachment and nurture that we have discussed previously are experienced in the settings in which the children are living and in the schools they attend. For this to happen requires adults who are confident enough to think about how to respond creatively in very distressing circumstances or who can offer comfort and support in the face of appalling behaviour. It also takes time – time in which a trusting relationship can be built through patience and the consistent provision of daily routines and ordinary experiences, such as going to bed, getting up in the morning, eating together and sharing activities. For teachers and schools, it means nurture groups!

BEING AFRAID TO SAY GOOD NIGHT

It is essential that teachers and social workers have a clear understanding of the importance of attachment and nurture. These should be core themes in education and training programmes at both qualifying and post qualifying levels. A developed understanding of the relational nature of their work is also vital in order to deliver specific interventions, e.g. nurture groups in schools, as well as for shaping the policy and organisational frameworks within which they operate.

However, the people who establish the closest relationships with children and young people in the course of their work are perhaps those often viewed as the least qualified of the professional cadre; namely, the foster carers and residential workers. It is these understated groups of people who are most directly affected by the pervasive and corrosive cultures of bureaucracy, fear and blame. In many local authorities, there are unbelievably large numbers of foster carers suspended as a result of allegations, often without a conclusive resolution to the subsequent investigation even after long periods of time. Occasionally these investigations drag out over a period of years, and one of the consequences is that the procedures of the investigation become the focus of attention, occupying accused and investigator alike, rather than the process leading to clarification and resolution of the original allegation or complaint.

We have described previously the ever-growing expectations on foster carers to receive advanced training and to record their work, i.e. their daily lives, in detail. And yet these are the people who really know the children and young people for whom they care, because they spend long periods of time with them in the closest of contact through the daily routines of ordinary family life. These routines may involve deeply personal tasks; for example, washing and bathing, the preparation and sharing of food at mealtimes, going to bed and getting up in the morning. How these activities are thought about and how they are provided for vulnerable, neglected or abused children is critical to their experience of what it means to be cared for and nurtured. If 'care' is to be something more than just the provision of shelter and food, it must include emotional warmth and a non-judgmental acceptance, both of which are essential for children's growth and development.

Foster carers, and residential staff for that matter, must feel confident in their role and feel free to offer the physical and emotional support the children demand in spontaneous and natural ways.

It is essential to have a thorough understanding of what is meant by 'safe care practice' and to realise that emotionally damaged or abused children might be hesitant or suspicious about being touched. Bath times or bed times are likely to produce anxiety, and meal times can trigger a deep sense of loss for the absence of good early nurturing. But understanding this does not substitute for the personal qualities and capacities required to be nurturing. It is also the case that 'safe care' cannot be provided if carers are worried about the consequences for saying good night by telling a bed time story in the child's bedroom when their training tells them to use a baby intercom. Likewise, natural care cannot be provided when a carer sitting on the sofa feels they must find a cushion to put between themselves and a child wanting to snuggle up!

Being able to offer natural care and affection in a stable and loving family environment, whilst at the same time having sufficient knowledge and skills to understand and respond to the underlying difficulties of each child and young person in need of foster care, demonstrates the complexities of the task facing foster carers. It is also part of the challenge for the workers and organisations that oversee their work.

Psychotherapy or other forms of individual therapy clearly have a part to play in helping some children. For the most part, however, their needs are likely to be best addressed in the context of supportive and nurturing relationships offered genuinely by adults who are truly caring and accepting and who are willing to take risks. In all these respects, social workers, teachers and other supporting workers share with direct carers the responsibilities that accompany such work, and they will similarly experience the personal impact that it may bring.

It is this shared responsibility to be meaningful and to re-establish the essential trust that is the basis of professional relationships, the ways in which different professional groups and agencies communicate with each other must be comprehensive and detailed. It is questionable whether the current ways devised to record and share information – manual or electronic – can do the job! In the next chapter, we look at the possibilities that using narrative approaches may bring to this debate and the importance of language as used by professionals to talk about their work and engage with the people they are trying to help and support.

Chapter 6

Why Tell Stories?

There's only one story, the story of your life.

John Ayre, Northrop Frye: *A Biography* (1989)

Two themes have reverberated constantly through this book: the importance of narrative and the way language is used to facilitate and describe work with vulnerable people. This chapter further considers how narrative thinking is particularly relevant where there may be risk of harm to children and young people, and how the way we use language as professional workers either distances us from the people we are trying to help or draws us into closer therapeutic relationships.

For as long as there has been communication between people, stories have been used to tell of important events, recount exciting or unusual experiences, and to describe the most profound of human endeavours. Telling stories is a distinctively human activity with roots to our history that are traceable through shared oral traditions and encapsulated in the passing on of memories through narrative. Understanding where we have come from and how things were in the past clarifies and gives meaning to our present circumstances and points us forward to a future.

We understand life sequentially; the process itself mirrors the way we know the human brain develops. We perceive reality in a narrative form; we look backwards, we think about what is happening to us now, and we look forward. We make connections; we look for causality and make use of symbols and metaphors to explain and describe our experience. Everyone has a story and everyone's story is different. As in the nurture-group evaluation project, using a narrative approach offered exciting opportunities for hearing what being in a nurture group meant to children, teachers and parents; and for including in the evaluation schema. It captured and enhanced understanding about the nurture-group experience in a way that other methods of data collection could not achieve.

THE PURPOSE OF NARRATIVE

We have a profound need to tell and hear stories. It is how we share experience, understand each other, and create community. Every con-

versation is full of personal anecdote; every effort to explain shared customs and values needs a tale; every bit of wisdom is best expressed by a story. The very way our minds think is the essence of story. So to master powerful and effective communication, to engage people and ensure they remember facts, or to break down barriers of isolation within or between groups, telling stories in some form is essential.

(Call of Story website)

Lucy Avraamidou and Jonathan Osborne (2008) refer to the work of Bruner who identifies two distinct ways in which human beings order experience. The first he calls 'paradigmatic', which refers to the use of reason and logic. The second way he refers to as 'narrative', and is concerned with the creation of stories.

As he (Bruner) described, narrative is used to refer to: a) a way of sculpting and structuring information through expressions of different media into readily understood forms that guide learners' comprehension; and b) a cognitive mode that learners use to make sense out of information or experience. Narrative then becomes part of how people understand the world in which they live and serves as a way of communicating that understanding to others.

(Avraamidou and Osborne 2008)

Avraamidou and Osborne conclude that '*stories then are a vehicle through which experiences and events are communicated amongst people.*' Narrative form gives a structure and meaning to the sharing of important events and experiences.

THE STRUCTURE OF NARRATIVE

There are a number of key elements that must be present for a narrative to work. There has to be purpose in the narrative – a meaning that can be discerned, even if it only emerges over time. There are events to be recounted, which connect with each other, and there is an overall structure with a beginning, middle and end. Through this structure, the events are related temporally, so narratives concern the past as well as the present and the future. There is agency; in other words, people who act and interact with each other, driving the narrative forward and making things happen, but also experiencing them as well. Finally, there must be a narrator and a listener. There is a critical relationship between the person telling their story and the person listening to it. The listener is the one who accepts the narrative, interprets it and shares its meaning with other people.

NARRATIVE IN ORGANISATIONAL STUDIES

Studies of organisational culture have been enriched through methodologies that have listened to and taken seriously narrative accounts of what it is like to work in particular organisations, and these accounts have been used to highlight specific aspects of corporate life. Working with ideas drawn from narrative approaches, researchers have been able to use the content of the stories they have heard to inform and deepen their understanding about ways of achieving successful organisational change, as well as to identify relevant material for staff training and development. Yiannis Gabriel comments in the introduction to his book, Storytelling in Organisations:

> By collecting stories in different organisations, by listening and comparing different accounts, by investigating how narratives are constructed around specific events, by examining which events in an organisation's history generate stories and which ones fail to do so, we gain access to deeper organisation realities, closely linked to their members' experiences. In this way, stories enable us to study organisational politics, culture and change in uniquely illuminating ways, revealing how wider organisational issues are viewed, commented upon and worked upon by their members.

(Gabriel 2000: 2)

One of the most valuable features of narrative is the opportunity it offers for collecting and collating the stories of extremely diverse groups of people. Such accounts often provide researchers with access to material that would not have been available within the usual parameters of research, and this allows minority voices to contribute to the general knowledge base about the real workings of particular organisations.

Understanding more about special events or crises that have occurred in the past, as well as knowing about the routine experiences of organisational life from the unique perspectives of individual members enhances the colour and texture of the overall picture. If stories are in the main told about 'heroes, villains and fools', then knowing which stories are related most frequently or repeated over long periods of time reveals important truths about an organisation's values and the kinds of behaviour that are genuinely respected or given weight in the decision making process. Carl Rhodes (1996) reports on a 'qualitative research approach to organisational change and learning based on the gathering and reporting of stories.' He emphasises the importance of narrative in considering diversity within organisations:

Storytelling is a research technique consistent with a pluralistic and diverse approach to organisational analysis. Rather than assuming that there is one reality as expressed by the singular and privileged authorial or managerial voice, stories taken from a variety of sources can provide an opportunity to see the inherent differences in how organisational members make sense of their organisational experience. Stories can "restore subjectivity to a terrain where it can be observed" (Gabriel, 1995, p. 498) and allow for an exposition of the intersubjectivity of organisational life based on the different personal experiences and sense making assumptions of organisational members.

(Carl Rhodes 1996)

NARRATIVE IN THERAPEUTIC WORK

The use of narrative in therapeutic work takes many varied forms. Some aspects of what has become known as 'life-story work' reflect the principles of narrative therapy whereby a child is encouraged to recount their life in a story form, trying to remember in sequence important experiences or recalling significant people in their lives through the years. Using a host of visual aids and objects that have meaning for the child, the adult worker helps them to think about events through their life.

One of the purposes of the therapy is to establish and strengthen the child's identity by increasing their feelings of self-worth, which may be very low indeed as is often the case for children with poor early learning and attachment experiences.

'Therapeutic story telling' builds upon the ancient tradition of telling stories to children. The indirect medium of narrative helps a child to think about themselves or take on board some unpalatable aspect of their reality without having to confront the trauma directly. The medium of the story offers the child opportunities to think about their feelings in different non-threatening ways that circumvent the defence of denial or the mechanisms that children use to block out voices they don't want to hear

(Sunderland 2009).

Alice Morgan explains the thinking behind narrative therapy and explores the different forms that it may take:

There are various principles which inform narrative ways of working, but in my opinion, two are particularly significant: always maintaining a stance of curiosity, and always asking questions to which you genuinely do not know the answers. I invite you to read this book with these two principles in mind. They inform the ideas, the stance, the tone, the values, the commitments and the beliefs of narrative therapy.

(Morgan, A. 2000: 2)

Morgan explains how narrative therapy involves listening to the story that each person want to tell about their lives. This story may be different from those that are usually told about them, and in order for this unique story to develop the therapist must build a trusting and confiding relationship with the individual. To facilitate this, it is necessary to ask questions to which 'you genuinely do not know the answers,' thereby permitting the individual to reframe their story for therapeutic benefit. The work is non-blaming and affirms the individual as the most important person in the telling of their particular story. For the most part, the direction of the therapy is lead by the person telling the story rather than the therapist, who is there to encourage and to prompt. Morgan summarises the main principles:

- Narrative therapy seeks to be a respectful, non-blaming approach to counselling and community work, which centres people as the experts in their own lives.

- It views problems as separate from people and assumes people have many skills, competencies, beliefs, values, commitments and abilities that will assist them to change their relationship with problems in their lives.

- Curiosity and a willingness to ask questions to which we genuinely don't know the answers are important principles of this work.

- There are many possible directions that any conversation can take (there is no single correct direction).

- The person consulting the therapist plays a significant part in determining the directions that are taken.

(ibid. 5)

As may be readily seen, the principles and values of narrative therapy resonate closely with those we have identified as critical for relational practice in work with children, young people and families, irrespective of the service area or agency focus. Whilst there is much more that could be said about the application of narrative approaches to both organisational and therapeutic settings, the reader is encouraged to pursue particular issues through the further reading and reference section. My purpose now is to take the ideas and principles identified above and show their relevance to the challenges posed for general mainstream practice across all areas of work with children, young people and families; for the organisations established to manage this work; and for those who create the policy framework within which they exist.

THE LANGUAGE OF MANAGERIALISM

The present day tendency towards managerialism and consumerism in social welfare and education services is reinforced by an overwhelming emphasis in policy that the primary role is social control and risk management. Both of these factors are reflected in the way language is used to record the activity of professional workers, whether through their inputs to electronic and manual data collection systems or to show how targeted outcomes are being achieved.

Gregory and Holloway comment: 'the language of risk management and the language of consumerism now dominate 'social work discourse.' They go on to pick up a point made in the introduction to this book: 'a good deal of the literature consists of 'how to' manuals with uncritical advice about processes such as risk assessment and management.' (Gregory and Holloway 2005: 46)

The growth of 'professionalism' and the associated ideas regarding expertise and specialist knowledge have contributed to the way language is used, which has served increasingly to distance workers from the people for whom the services are intended. Establishing and developing relationships is not necessary for managerial purposes; neither is it desirable, nor perhaps even possible, if the task is defined in terms of monitoring people's behaviour to make actuarial risk assessments about their potential for future offending. The belief that the job has been done once necessary data has been inputted and the results show that targets have been achieved – or that the specified number of sessions have been delivered or requisite number of visits have been made (at least by someone) – creates remarkably unstable and unsafe work environments. This contributes little to the protection and safety of vulnerable people. As Ronald Doctor reminded us, the kind of work we are talking about, engaging with vulnerable or potentially dangerous people, must take place within a containing framework of support and supervision.

NARRATIVE AND RELATIONSHIPS

One of the values of narrative is that individual stories should be told in the unique voice of the narrator. This means that the person telling the narrative retains control over the content and direction of the story. Equally important, however, is the response of the person who listens to and hears the evolving narrative. In other words, a relationship is implied in the very act of telling a story or recounting a narrative. We are relational creatures: our most important early learning experiences come through the relationship established with our primary carer, and the quality of that attachment significantly shapes our later ability to make and sustain relationships with others. The most effective models of intervention are those based on relational approaches and see the development of a relationship as the ground for behavioural change and personal growth.

But as I have argued, in order to be effective these approaches need to be contained within a framework that understands and supports the task, and time, continuity and stability at all levels are pre-requisites.

USE OF NARRATIVE IN CHILD PROTECTION

Visiting and engaging families who may be hostile or even threaten violence is a daunting prospect. Establishing a relationship of trust in the face of such difficulties is clearly complex and demanding. It is not surprising that being able to fall back on simplistic or purely mechanistic forms for recording visits to troublesome families is, unconsciously at least, welcome relief for hard-pressed workers. The pervasive fear of making a mistake and the consequences of being blamed complete the ingredients for producing nervous, hesitant practice with insight neither looked for nor valued.

Indeed, as has been shown in various enquiry reports following harrowing incidents of abuse or child deaths, the failure of the network of professional workers to sustain meaningful contact with vulnerable families and to understand and interpret their unfolding narrative of events has been, on occasions, catastrophic. Nevertheless, whilst it is clearly important to be able to gather information over periods of time and from different settings, this information requires analysis and thinking about in ways that enable the discrete inputs of different agencies and disciplines to be brought together to provide a comprehensive account of what is going on. Using narrative, which encourages the unique stories of each protagonist to be told in an environment of supportive and encouraging relationships, may suggest a more fruitful way forward.

Making connections, being curious and knowing what questions to ask – preferably ones to which the answer is not known – are essential skills not only for individual workers but at the organisational level as well. The DCSF report on Serious Case Reviews, *'Analysing child deaths and serious injury through abuse and neglect'* (RR023) makes salutary reading. In the face of current pressures and demands made on social workers, but also on other professional workers, the report states clearly:

> *To have a better chance of understanding the risks of harm that children face, practitioners should be encouraged to be curious and to think critically and systematically.*

(ibid. 2)

Commenting on the use of the Common Assessment Framework, the report concludes:

> *Much of the practice described in the serious case reviews is static. Too often, the Assessment Framework appears to be used in a flat, non-dynamic way. This leads to the accumulation of facts but little appreciation of how to formulate the facts in the manner of a clear explanation (rather than a dense description). Theoretically informed explanations are able to accommodate and make sense of what might otherwise appear to be a simple accumulation of facts. They guide observations. They sponsor curiosity and new lines of enquiry. They offer a framework and a language that enable different professional groups to communicate and recognise the value of sharing information helping to deepen the case formulation.*

(ibid. 63)

In seeking appropriate *'theoretically informed explanations'*, it is surely not too fanciful to claim that attachment and nurturing provide sufficiently rigorous models for thinking about the material that emerges from 'observations' and out of continuous and stable relationships between workers and families. Writing about these relationships and recounting their different narratives in ways that provide *'clear explanations'* rather than *'dense descriptions'* is a challenge for all professional workers, but it is not impossible. Whilst it is not being suggested that writing a report becomes akin to writing a novel, or that case notes become over elaborate diaries, it is surely critical for formats used in case recording include some facility for recording sequences of events and opportunities for recording thinking and reflection.

TWO CASE STUDIES

The case study, *The Boy Who Knew Too Much*, was shared with me by a foster carer. It tells of his family's experience when they fostered a boy who had many needs and whose early life was obviously less than satisfactory. It reflects the complexity that much of our work presents, and the ambivalence of feelings that we all share. The second case study, *When Adam Became Eve*, is an account of the life of a therapeutic community for young people over a 12 month period during which the staff group, the young people's group and the whole community together had to live alongside a young person struggling with issues of identity. The challenges this presented put the principles upon which the community had been built to a profound test. The narrator is the director.

A careful reading of these narratives will provide examples from lived experience of a number of the themes explored throughout this book, in particular the importance of the six principles of nurture and the need for maintaining thinking during times of uncertainty.

The Boy Who Knew Too Much

'How long is he likely to be with us?' As with so many children in foster care, we had no idea how long fourteen-year-old Richard was going to be a part of our family. We had only been foster carers for a few months and our only previous 'placement' as these children seemed to be called by the professionals had stayed with us for just about two weeks before going off somewhere. I wish I could say where Charlene, as we called the little ten-year-old girl who stayed with us, went to live; but we weren't told, and despite asking we somehow never found out.

In fact, Richard lived with us for just over three years, and we helped him move on from living with us to what they called 'independent living' just after his seventeenth birthday. I can't say it was all straightforward, but in life nothing ever is; and it certainly wasn't for Richard – or for us for that matter! Living with Richard was just about the hardest thing that my wife Helen and I have ever had to do. Even now, some five years later, writing this account and thinking back to the sleepless nights when we were waiting for the police to call or remembering the holiday that we cut short when Richard threw a tantrum in the resort shop, brings a shudder down my spine. On the other hand, I can also remember the incredible sadness we felt when Richard's father died, and we had to tell him and take him to the funeral, even though 'contact' had always been traumatic. And I can remember laughing a lot as well and enjoying doing things that we hadn't done since our own children had grown up and left home.

Of course, he had always found other people hard-going, and it is no surprise to Helen and I that Richard lives alone in a small flat. But he is working, still in the taxi office doing his five shifts a week – not in prison or another institution – and I think that counts as success.

We don't see him as often now, but we never know when the phone might ring. We learned as much from Richard as we hope he did from us: not to blame; the importance of just being there at times when we wanted to give up and thought we couldn't take any more; and in the end, to believe that despite an awful start in life, there can be a more hopeful future.

RICHARD'S ARRIVAL TO LIVE WITH US

As I said, we didn't know very much about Richard. We were initially contacted by Margaret, our link social worker, from the independent fostering agency that we worked for. They are a small, friendly agency – a nice group of people who supported us very well. Margaret told us that there was a fourteen-year-old boy who had been in a residential unit for a couple of years, but who had had to leave and his local authority was looking for a foster placement. The agency believed the placement might become long term, and Margaret and her manager thought that we might be suitable. We also had a vacancy!

Helen and I had been foster carers for about four months, having completed our assessment and been to Panel. The assessment, which Margaret did, was a real eye-opener for both Helen and me. We had had a pretty ordinary life, or so we thought; I had been a teacher and taken early retirement, whilst Helen had worked as a secretary both before and after our two children were born. By the time Richard came to live with us, both Alan and Sophie had grown up and moved away. Alan was in the army at the time and is still serving, whilst Sophie (also a teacher) had moved out to live with her boyfriend to whom she is now married.

What the assessment did was make us think more about how we had grown up, and it was something of a surprise to find out that Helen had suffered abuse as a child. She had never told me about what her uncle had done, and neither had she told her parents, both of whom were now dead. We talked a lot about that and about the death of her parents, who had died over ten years ago but within a very short time of each other. Helen's mother had been diabetic and her father had cancer. Although at the time of their deaths we had talked, we realised as Margaret spoke to us that we had not really grieved and had just been too busy with all the arrangements and trying to comfort our children. My parents were also dead; my father died when I was fifteen and my mother just before my fiftieth birthday, some five years before the fostering assessment.

Whilst we knew very little about Richard, we were excited about the possibility of looking after him. We wanted a long-term placement and although we had no idea what that meant, it was one of the categories for which we had been approved by the Panel. We just wanted some stability for the child we were to look after, and I suppose for ourselves as well. Too much change didn't seem like a good thing and we had always thought children should enjoy the benefits of consistency and knowing where they stood.

We felt nervous and apprehensive, wondering whether we would cope or be good enough and what sort of boy Richard would be. At that time, I think we were more worried about us than about Richard, and I am pretty certain that we didn't think enough about how he might be feeling! Now, with hindsight and having spoken to Richard in the years that were to come, I know that he felt just the same as we did – but even more so! For Richard, the feelings were: 'Is this going to last? Is it worth making an effort, or will they do as all the others have done and give up? Why should I bother?' Later, he couldn't even describe the anger he felt at the time, and I think neither he nor we have ever understood the envy and the rage that he felt when he saw us, came into our home and eventually met our children.

BACKGROUND

The information about Richard's early life has always been patchy and even now I am not sure we know the full story. Richard himself has always been reluctant to talk too much about what he can remember, and we felt uncertain about how far we should probe. On the whole, we just did what we could and responded as best we thought to whatever was happening in the here and now. We knew from reports and from our few meetings with his natural father that Richard's mother had been seriously diabetic and prone to collapsing as she was unable to manage her insulin. We were never sure why this should be so, whether it was because she had other problems or perhaps learning difficulties; but we did know that from an incredibly early age, Richard had to learn to ring for an ambulance and to give his mum something sweet! Richard's father, who we met on a few occasions before he too died, had obviously had a drink problem and had already left the home when Richard's mother died. At the time, Richard was just four years old.

Richard went to a number of foster homes but was finally adopted just before his sixth birthday. The adoptive parents, in their early thirties, had not been able to have children. They were both professional people, well off, and keen to adopt. Richard was with them for nearly five years and it seemed that everything was going reasonably well, although from the reports it did look as if he was providing them with a number of problems, particularly at school.

Then, miraculously, the wife conceived and there was a newborn baby in the family. It is hard to know what exactly happened, but within a year of the birth the adoption came to an end. There was some information that suggested the parents thought Richard might harm the baby, but there was no hard evidence that we could find, and again Richard has always been silent about what happened and how he felt about the breakdown with his adoptive family.

There were further foster placements after this, but also quite a few changes of social worker as well, so there did not appear to us to have been any continuity for Richard or any way of getting the whole picture together for him. We tried whilst Richard was with us, but had little success.

From the age of twelve to about thirteen and a half, Richard found himself in what was called a specialist residential therapeutic community. Whilst with us, Richard talked positively about this placement and in particular about some of the staff whom he clearly liked and who were kind to him and took an interest in his life. Unfortunately, Richard found it very hard to make friends with the other young people in the community and those he did link up with were a delinquent sub-group.

Increasing involvement in various forms of theft, burglary and stealing cars climaxed in Richard being part of a group that one night set fire to some outbuildings. Although it was acknowledged that Richard was peripheral to the actual arson, it was decided that his placement should come to an end.

The reports from the therapeutic community were the most extensive we have ever seen on Richard, although we were only allowed to see them when he was about to leave us. The psychiatric report commented on his early deprivation and lack of attachment being at the root of his problems in forming relationships and what was described as his 'chaotic ambivalence towards other people', especially adults.

We thought that seemed about right. To us, he was old before his time – at times incredibly adult in his responses, but at other times just like a very small child, except he had never experienced a normal early childhood and didn't seem to know what to do with toys – although he loved having them. Richard remains quite bitter about the ending of this placement and still tries from to time to find out where some of the staff are living and what they are doing, although the community has been closed for a number of years.

ISSUES FOR FOSTERING

I don't think we shall ever forget our first meeting with Richard. There had been no chance for us to visit him or for him to come to our house to see us.

It all had to happen at once as there had been some problem in the foster home where he was staying. Richard was a slightly podgy boy of average height with a shock of ginger hair and glasses, but with an infectious smile that he turned on us as he came in with his social worker. The social worker was called Joe, and he had been Richard's social worker for a few months. Although he did not really know Richard, we liked him and were very lucky because he stayed Richard's social worker all the time he was with us and we could not have wanted for better support.

Richard was wary of us at first, but within a matter of days had become almost over friendly and was confiding in us about how terrible things had been in his last foster home. Of course, we were delighted and began to think that we were probably rather good at this fostering business. In particular, he seemed much attached to me, wanting to know if he could call me dad; but towards my wife, he was somewhat distant, calling her Helen in a rather dismissive way. Of course, as time went on we learned more about what this might be about, and how Richard was very adept at playing us off against each other. He had a way of asking us questions about each other that suggested he knew something more than he was telling, and that it would be damaging or detrimental to our relationship if he revealed all.

Although over time we could see what was happening, it was still insidious and on occasions it left Helen and me unsure about each other and how we should respond to Richard's probing. In the end, we decided the best approach was just to be open, and if he asked or suggested something we would immediately confront it by bringing the other person into the conversation.

We became aware of the same sort of thing happening with our wider family, including Alan and Sophie. In the early months of Richard's stay with us, our relationship with Sophie was a bit strained. We weren't terribly happy with her choice of partner and thought she was rushing into the relationship. We were careful not to talk about this in front of Richard, but somehow he knew; and with a well chosen and suitably timed remark, usually in front of Sophie, he could generate an argument which he seemed to enjoy watching. It took a couple of years before the relationships between us all settled down and for Alan and Sophie to really take to Richard or accept him as part of the family. Even now, whilst they ask after him and would do anything to help him, there is a feeling of suspicion which Richard reciprocates.

It is hard to think about this; of course, Richard might have been jealous of our children and I suppose they had similar feelings towards him. Despite being older, I wonder if they thought that somehow Richard was getting a better deal from Helen and me than they had received. I suppose you can never really know these things, but what I do know is that whilst Richard was living with us we lost our previous social life and quite a few friends. Being with Richard was all consuming!

As I look back through the collection of monthly reports we had to produce for our link social worker and the agency, it reads like a roller coaster. Quiet months are reflected by such comments as 'Richard did well in school,' 'Much better behaviour at home, getting on better with Helen'. Of course, the difficulties are there as well, but overall the record does seem to reflect what we both now feel: that over the three years or so, we did make progress, and we came to see Richard as part of the family and still do.

It didn't always feel like that, however. The challenges were considerable. There were the one-off events, like the time we went on holiday. Richard hadn't wanted to go; I am not sure why. But he was argumentative before we left for the caravan site, obstructive and rude during the journey, and then when we arrived he went off and we couldn't find him for over three hours. Finally, he turned up in the camp shop. We found out after we received a visit from the site manager telling us that Richard had been arrested for shoplifting. As we went across to the shop, we could hear Richard swearing loudly at the staff. When we went in, he did manage to control himself for about five minutes – and then started swearing again, this time at us. I could feel myself getting angry and embarrassed; we had been coming to this site for years and knew everyone. In the end, we managed to get Richard back to our caravan and into the car. Holiday: over. We never found out why he was so determined that the holiday wouldn't happen.

This sort of thing happened a few times – not as serious as missing a holiday, but real tantrums and behaviour that seemed much more like that of a much younger child. Meal times in the early months were also difficult. Sometimes Richard wouldn't want to eat with us or with anyone else for that matter. He had to have his food specially prepared and needed to know how it had been cooked. Margaret was helpful over this issue, pointing out to us that children who had not received much love early on in their lives sometimes found food and mealtimes really difficult. Trying to force the issue seemed to make things worse, and in the end we tried to adopt a tolerant attitude, letting things happen at his pace and in his time, which seemed to work.

More difficult to cope with was the behaviour that developed as he reached sixteen. He got in with another delinquent group of slightly older young-people who he met through school. This group were into cars; some of the older youths had their own and Richard enjoyed riding around with them, despite our best efforts to warn him of the possible consequences. Staying out late became a norm, and then we found out that as well as driving their own cars, the group were stealing cars and joy riding. On one occasion, the police brought Richard home in the early hours saying that he had been picked up in a stolen car – not driving, but a passenger. The result of this was more involvement with social workers, this time from a Youth Offending Team.

A feature of our time with Richard was the way that it seemed some things would always remain a mystery to us. He was needy, often clingy and some-times it seemed really obsessed with what Helen and I were doing or thinking about.

At other times, he was distant towards us, going out when he wanted and getting into trouble. Although we had experience of teenage behaviour, and I had been a teacher, there was definitely something different about Richard. It wasn't just normal adolescent behaviour; he really didn't seem to know who he was, and we knew little about what was going on inside his head.

Perhaps the thing that shook us up most was the death of Richard's father, which happened two years after he first came to live with us. We had met Richard's father on two occasions, and Richard had been very ambivalent about this contact. Apparently the legal position was that Richard could choose whether or not he wanted to see his dad, and there would be months without any contact at all – no letters or phone calls. Then, out of the blue, there would be a call; and twice these ended up with a meeting.

Richard and his father met in a cafe near where his dad was living, and I went along because the social worker thought it would be a good idea. Richard showed all the disinterest a fifteen year old can muster, and yet there was something that he desperately wanted from those meetings; but whatever it was, he didn't seem to get it as we came away both times feeling frustrated and with a sense that something was wrong. After these contacts, Richard became even more clinging towards us; but at the same time he seemed to want to do more in the home, almost as if he wanted to look after us or make sure that Helen and I were ok.

We learned about the death of Richard's father from Joe, his social worker. Apparently he had drunk himself into a stupor, walked out of his block of flats and fallen in front of a bus. Richard's reaction was surprisingly very matter-of-fact. He didn't cry, but just said, 'Now I am really on my own.' We felt we wanted to do more to comfort him, but weren't sure what we could do. We took Richard to the funeral, which was a miserable affair. In fact, we were the only ones there – and despite the best efforts of a very kind vicar, we all felt terrible and very sad, almost lonely. When Helen and I talked about this later, we both knew that whilst we were trying to care for Richard we had been thinking about our parents and our losses, and we were glad that during our assessment we had had the chance to think about these things in some detail.

THE PROFESSIONAL NETWORK

One of the things that we found most difficult in being foster carers was the number of people who needed to be involved in what we thought of as our normal daily life, and their apparently insatiable appetite for meetings. Even more galling was the fact that we did not seem to be needed at a number of these meetings – and even when we did go, we felt most times that our views were not really wanted or taken seriously. I could never work out why that should be? After all, as a teacher I had attended numerous meetings, and thought I knew the protocols that apply when professionals convene meetings.

Individually we found most of the professionals involved with Richard to be helpful and understanding; Margaret from the fostering agency and Joe the social worker in particular. Richard's school were also supportive and put up with a lot from him when with other pupils I suspect they might not have been so tolerant! But, when they came together and were joined by the independent reviewing officer, Joe's senior social worker (and her manager), the educational psychologist from Richard's school, the clinical psychologist and the psychiatrist from the CAMHS team, the specialist teacher from the looked-after children team, and the YOT workers, it all got a bit too much.

From our point of view, these meetings never seemed to get to grips with what we thought at the time to be the key issues. There was a lot of talk about planning for independence, although we thought Richard was very dependent, and there was a lot of talk about conduct disorder. We wanted to know more about what we could do to help, but somehow we never got to this discussion. The educational psychologist was the most helpful. She talked about what might have happened to Richard when he was younger, living with his mother who was unable to care for him properly and who, in fact, putt a lot of responsibility on him for her care at a time he needed to be nurtured and looked after. That seemed to make sense of why he was so changeable, at times seeking affection from us in an almost overbearing way, whilst at other times he could be defiant and on occasions aggressive, particularly towards Helen.

Another thing that struck us at these meetings was the way people talked about Richard seemed to de-personalise him. It appeared from the discussions that he was more of a syndrome or a set of problems than a young boy. The YOT team talked about an emerging offender profile, whilst one of the psychiatrists talked of personality disorder. We didn't understand what this kind of talk was leading to, but didn't think it fitted what we knew about Richard and what we thought his behaviour was about.

The way Richard appeared to deal with the breakdown with his adoptive family is a good example of what seemed to us to be his contradictory nature. Whilst he was with us, and despite the fact that he had not seen his adoptive parents for nearly five years, he talked a great deal about them. Sometimes this would be in very positive terms, remembering the big presents he had received from them on birthdays or at Christmas, the luxury of their house, or the exciting trips out and the treats that had accompanied them. He would rather cuttingly compare these material benefits with our lifestyle and the 'rubbish' that we offered him! We tried to deal with this sensibly, but at times we were irritated by the comparisons and felt a bit of 'If you liked it so much and they were so great, then why did it all break down – and perhaps you would like to go back there?' Fortunately we didn't ever say it, but it did get to us. On the other hand, he expressed no desire to see them and quite often after yet another eulogy about their wealth, he would revert to being clingy towards us.

Perhaps he was letting us know that although he couldn't say it, he knew that we provided him with something different – or perhaps he wanted just to wind us up even more?

Before going to the therapeutic community, Richard had received a statement of special education needs, which meant that when he came to live with us he could go the local day EBD School. This was real bonus for us, as they seemed to understand about Richard and what he needed in school. In fact, Richard was a bright boy and we often thought that in normal circumstances he would have done well in school. He liked going, although he had no interest in the work that they wanted him to do, preferring to draw or use the computer to look at anything to do with cars. The teachers thought he was clever but lacked confidence, and they reported to us on various occasions that after producing a piece of work for which he received praise, he would tear it up, throw it away and go into one of his tantrums.

What the school did seem to provide for Richard was the opportunity to be normal. This might seem a funny thing to say, and I can't put it any other way: one of the things we noticed about Richard was that he desperately wanted to be thought of as just another young person; but at another level he knew that he wasn't and that he couldn't cope with many of the situations that other young people faced on a daily basis. Making friends is a good example of what I mean. Richard had hardly any friends and when he did seem to be friendly with another young person, something always seemed to happen that meant that the friendship didn't last.

Whilst with us, he never had a girlfriend or seemed to have any interest in girls. We were aware of reports from the therapeutic community that he had been found with other older boys in 'compromising sexual behaviour' as they called it, but which they thought – and we agreed – was probably just experimental behaviour and a seeking for some kind of comfort and release. I remember one conversation with him when he asked about AIDS and what did I think about it? I took a fairly factual line, but wondered what he was really asking me about, and as we talked I thought he was sounding out my views about what I thought of homosexuals.

People's reactions to Richard were incredibly varied but never neutral. Some people really liked him and seemed almost fascinated by his behaviour and apparent maturity. He could certainly hold a conversation and he had that knack of saying what the other person appeared to want to hear. In particular, he could ask questions that hinted at knowing more than he really did about them, and thus he could draw out some confidence which he enjoyed using at a later date as an opportunity to share a secret with someone else! Other people seemed to take an instant dislike to Richard; we sometimes thought they were perhaps afraid of him, sensing some underlying potential for malevolence or thinking that he knew something that could be used to hurt them.

We experienced both of these feelings at different times, although as we came to know him, we saw through some of his outward behaviour and realised that really we were looking after a rather vulnerable little boy who had seen and done things, and had things done to him, that were way beyond his years; and that if only we could have cared for him when he was younger and for longer then perhaps we might have been able to do more.

MOVING ON TO INDEPENDENT LIVING

We had been told in our training to be foster carers that any ending of a placement would be difficult for us and also for the child or young person we were looking after. The social workers started talking about independent living before Richard had turned sixteen, although we could see little evidence that he was ready for this. Some new workers from the Independent Living team joined the other professionals and they told us we should make sure we were preparing Richard for independence: helping him to budget and manage his money, and to travel alone and be able to look after himself, such as cooking meals and doing his laundry. Most of these things did not seem to us to be particularly difficult; we were more worried about how he would live on his own without friends.

We assured him that he could always call us or visit and that we would stay in touch. Richard's attitude was, as ever, what I suppose you would call ambivalent. At the meetings he was enthusiastic and positive about living independently, seeing it as a way of achieving the 'normality' he craved for. To us at home, he was a combination of anger – as if somehow we were turning him out – and anxiety, worried about how he would manage.

The independent living turned out to be a hostel, with minimum adult supervision, located right across the other side of town from where we lived and where he went to school. Richard had his own room but shared facilities with five other young people. He had a place at a local college, and we hoped that he would find there the support he needed.

At first we had little contact from Richard. We had decided that we would leave it to him to contact us and tried to be clear that he could call us whenever. Joe collected him and his belongings on the day he moved out, a few months after his seventeenth birthday, and we said goodbye as cheerfully as we could.

FINAL THOUGHTS

It is now five years since Richard moved out from our home. We did not really foster again after he left us. We had a couple of younger children on a respite basis, but I think we both felt that we couldn't commit to another young person; it was more the emotional drain that we felt rather than anything else.

Richard didn't contact us at all for about a year, but since then we have seen him in the town and he calls us on the phone from time to time. He has visited us occasionally, and we had a good night out for his twenty-first birthday.

It's so hard to say what we feel about the time Richard was with us and since he has left. He was so needy, he really was a little boy who knew too much and had so many experiences that hurt him. We tried once to count up the number of adults who had been involved in his life, but we couldn't manage it – the number just seemed to grow. We are left with a sense that we did our best; we stayed the course as best we could and didn't give up. But did we succeed? How could we 'evaluate the placement' as we were asked to do shortly after he left us? Did he ever tell us how he felt, or did we just hear what we wanted to hear? Did we love him enough? There really are more questions than answers.

AND RICHARD'S REFLECTIONS

I have been asked to give my point of view on what John has written. I don't want to say much, but John and Helen were good to me and I still think about them, more than about anybody else I suppose. I am doing OK now. I've got my flat and a job, but I still feel lonely and miss people. John and Helen gave me a home and they didn't kick me out, even though I probably deserved it. I wish I could have stayed with them, but I don't think I could have; and I thought that poxy hostel would be better than it was. But I like my flat and I've got a few mates at the taxi firm. I know that I can call John and Helen whenever I want to, and that's good enough for now.

When Adam Became Eve

The London Therapeutic Community (LTC) was established through a partnership of a voluntary organisation, with a distinguished history of providing therapeutic care for damaged young people and London local authorities. The aim of the project was to provide a residential, therapeutic service for young people aged 16-21 years. This was on the basis that there was no provision of this type in London and that there were identifiable numbers of young people who on reaching their sixteenth birthday were not ready to engage with independent living or able to cope with the type of accommodation and limited support available.

The principles upon which the LTC was founded were drawn from the tradition of therapeutic communities and focused on understanding and exploring the group dynamics arising from the daily life of a community of staff and young people living and working alongside each other. The programme was created around a series of educational activities, encouraging young people to participate in age appropriate tasks and gain accredited awards, whilst recognising that many of them had not achieved in their previous educational experiences and had a negative view about education and a poor sense of their own worth and abilities.

THE DAILY PROGRAMME

The daily routines were central to the life of the community; getting up and having breakfast together; a morning planning meeting and then activities followed by lunch; a main community meeting of young people and staff was convened before further small groups and activities through the afternoon completed the day. The evening meal was prepared by the staff and young people together and was preceded by a shopping trip to spend the allocated budget for the day or once a week for the 'big shop'. Evening activities were planned with a group option or on an individual basis as negotiated. Settling the community at night was a demanding task but one to which considerable thought was given in order to achieve the balance between meeting the individual needs of very anxious young people for whom the night could hold terror and ensuring that group expectations about young people being in their own rooms and getting some sleep were met, at least most of the time!

Young people were supported by staff to keep their own rooms tidy and clean with some help given to the cleaning of communal areas. Whilst lunch was prepared and cooked, other meals were the responsibility of the staff and young people who managed the budget for this. The budget also included money for cleaning materials and other domestic necessities.

THE STAFF GROUP

The staff group were recruited from a range of professional disciplines, including social work, mental health nursing, teaching and youth work. A few staff had no professional qualification but experience of working with young people in residential settings. The gender balance was around half and half. The structure of the staff group was a director, 3 assistant directors, 4 senior workers and ten therapeutic workers. There was an Administrative team of 3 people, a cook, a cleaner and a handyman. The staff team was supported by a clinical psychologist (2 days per week) a psychiatrist (1 day per week) and a psychotherapist (2 days per week). Staff could book time with the 'consultants' to discuss issues to do with young people for whom they were allocated as key workers and also received supervision on a monthly basis through the line management system. The whole staff team met weekly for an afternoon, which included a detailed presentation by a key worker on the programme and progress of one of the young people. There were also twice daily handover meetings.

THE YOUNG PEOPLE'S GROUP

Over time the young people's group grew to 15 in total. At the time Steven came to the community there were another 12 young people in the group and during his stay another 2 young people joined. It was expected that young people would be funded to stay for at least 2 years, but achieving this was a constant battle. However, in a number of instances the degree of difficulty presented by the young people meant that other placement options were not viable or the level of risk they posed in the wider community was so high that the required level of supervision could only be achieved within a residential setting.

The young people presented over a range of different spectrums including aspergers, conduct disorders and emerging mental health issues. All of them had previous residential experiences including for some periods of time in psychiatric units or secure accommodation. It was not a delinquent group although one or two had some previous minor offences on their record. The group always had more boys than girls and during Steven's time there was a group of 4 young women in the community. Although most activities were mixed and open to all the community, there were specific groups for the young women and young men, and the girls had their own living area to which they and the female staff usually gravitated in the evening.

The therapeutic programme was centred on group work, with the focus being the daily community meeting, chaired by the director. Other small groups also met and each young person had a key worker and opportunities for individual time on a planned, regular basis. Regular case review meetings involving the young person's local authority provided the basis for future planning and monitoring of each young person's progress within the community programme.

Although each young person had their own unique history and story to tell there were a number of themes that consistently cropped up and became topics of interest in the life of the community. The work of the therapeutic community was built on the relationships between adults and young people and within these groups. Establishing trust and openness was crucial in order that the young people might experience the adults around them in a different way to how adults had been towards them previously, which was likely to have been abusive or neglectful. In the context of becoming safer and more secure within the community young people were more able to talk about their experiences and to find alternative and better ways to live for the future. So, relationships became a number one issue; this was often seen in discussion about favouritism, especially if detected or thought to exist in the director's behaviour towards any individual young person or member of staff for that matter. Pairing was strongly discouraged; although inevitable, any indication that young people were pairing up was immediately highlighted and brought to a community meeting. More usual were discussions about events or incidents that had occurred and the meaning of these for the whole community. Young people came to be able to talk about their lives, often very powerfully and movingly, within the community meetings, each one at a different level although for some this remained difficult throughout their stay.

As may be imagined life was never dull, it was often fraught and with a highly charged emotional content. These were young people who were able to make their feelings known, not immediately with thoughtful words but often with extreme acting out, including self-harming or aggression towards others, virulent and deeply personal verbal abuse aimed at each other and staff and deviant, destructive acts of hostility towards the community. Not many will forget the faeces in the saucepan just before supper!!

STEVEN'S ARRIVAL

At the time Steven joined LTC the community had been running for about 2½ years. Most of the early 'testing out' by the first group of young people had subsided and the staff group had stabilised. Routines were in place and the community had begun to talk about itself recognising a past against which to compare the present. The community meetings were being regularly attended and often provided a forum for lively and useful discussions whilst staff meetings had an established agenda. There were some important rituals in place to support the daily and weekly activities and the staff group was more confident about their role and the nature of the work.

Steven was an attractive boy of just 16 years and of Anglo-Indian appearance. He had long eye lashes which he used to both ingratiate himself with staff and flirt with young people, both the girls and the boys. He was charming, but provocative. He also had a temper which could escalate into violence; on one occasion he threw a kettle of hot water towards a male member of staff, not aiming to hit but certainly to scare.

He came from a children's home from which he had been excluded for violent behaviour and there were no family members involved with his care or with whom he was in contact. Information about his earlier life was sketchy; it was reported he had come from India at about 9 years old, sent over by his family but to whom and for what purpose was never clear. He moved through a succession of children's homes, had frequent changes of social worker and it was very difficult to collate any consistent or detailed account of his life. Steven, himself, was unforthcoming about the early part of his life although over time a few, key 'facts' were revealed.

REACTIONS TO STEVEN

As might be expected reactions to Steven were mixed and strong. Amongst the young people he became something of a favourite with the girls, to whom he was attractive and non-threatening. The boys were much more ambivalent and regarded him with suspicion and on occasions with outright hostility. He seemed to present them with a challenge about their own identity as if by being unsure about Steven's sexuality they feared the worst for themselves, particularly if they appeared to like him or were seen too close in his company.

Within the staff group the reactions went along similar tracks. The female staff on the whole found him amusing, clever and interesting. He did well in his studies and was affectionate around the women staff, seeking them out and looking for physical contact. The men were much more ambivalent and 'split' around their reactions. His male key worker, also and coincidentally of Anglo-Indian origin, established with Steven what appeared to be a close and confiding relationship. Steven spent time in his company and began to share some of his thoughts and feelings, at first about superficial matters but later on more personal information began to emerge. Other male staff were definitely more wary around Steven and introduced quite early on into the staff meetings suggestions that perhaps he was not suitable for LTC and that another placement might be better suited to his needs. After the incident of the thrown kettle this pressure increased with anxious demands to the management team as to "What are you going to do about him?"

Over about six months Steven gradually seemed to settle into the community and found his place with both staff and young people. Then there came a change in his behaviour. His original camp behaviours escalated around the community as did his need for physical contact, touching and holding hands becoming commonplace. He also began to 'abscond', staying out over night and then for longer periods, two or three days at a time. No-one could find out where he was going although thoughts about male prostitution were voiced amongst the staff. On returning from his absences Steven was tired, ate and then went to bed. His going missing was discussed in the community meeting and received with comments such as "Good" from a section of the boys' group to "What are you doing about it?" and "It's your fault" addressed to everyone, from the girls.

Then one night, about three o'clock in the morning, a knock at the front door of the community building was answered by a member of staff who found himself facing a young woman asking to be let in. Taking a closer look he saw to his utter amazement that it was Steven. Without much more discussion Steven came in and went to his bedroom. The next morning he appeared at breakfast dressed in girls' clothing and with liberally, if rather unskilfully, smeared make-up on his eyes and lips. He appeared to have grown breasts which on inspection (or rather, discreet looking) turned out to be a pair of stuffed socks put under his vest. Steven announced that from now on he was a girl and was to be called Sharon. To say he caused a stir is somewhat of an understatement although, after the initial consternation, breakfast continued and the group moved towards the morning meeting!

MORE REACTIONS

It would be an overstatement to say that from that morning meeting until the time Steven left LTC, just over a year later, there was only topic of conversation. However, his presence did affect much of what was said and done in and by the community. The reactions in the staff and young people's groups followed for the most part their already delineated views about Steven, although the differences were sharpened and more intense.

For the staff group it became clear that however 'hot' the issue might be it was important for both Steven and the rest of the group to contain the explosive feelings that were emerging and to try and be as 'matter-of- fact' as possible about things. At the same time it was essential to make sure that Steven had opportunities to talk and receive support from trusted adults within the community. A central, contentious issue was the decision as to by what name he should be known. Some staff, mainly but not universally the women, felt he should be called Sharon as a mark of respect for his wishes and to encourage him in whatever future direction he might take. Others felt that whilst he should not be prevented from wearing female clothing he should continue to be called Steven, to maintain a sense of proportion and reality! In the end he remained Steven to the staff group. The consultant group were helpful at this time to both the staff group and to Steven as well as they talked with him and identified other more specialist resources to help with the possible longer-term consequences of whatever decision he might wish to make. That is not to say that there were no disagreements or strongly voiced opinions within the staff team. What remained essential was the availability of time for the staff to talk together, openness for the expression of feelings about the situation and individual space for reflection about the meaning and implications of what was happening. For the community as a whole, living with the deeply uncomfortable feelings that Steven evoked in everyone, was a test of the established culture of the community for being accepting and non-judgemental and a benchmark for its future capacity to be a safe and secure base for the young people.

For the young people, Steven's apparent transition to Sharon was especially problematic. The girls were encouraging and continued to 'pet' him; on occasions they tried to assimilate him into their group although at other times they would distance themselves from him and seek the company of the female staff, huddling together in their own living area. The boys were either directly hostile to Steven or tried to appear unaffected. In individual sessions they talked a lot about him, asking questions about what was going to happen, some of them clearly anxious that the community was not going to be able to survive what they considered to be an onslaught on its very being!

Over a period of a few months things did begin to settle down. The structure of the daily routines and the regular opportunities for issues to be raised and discussed in community meetings both contained the anxiety and allowed it to be expressed. Steven's absences from the community reduced in frequency and in the length of time he stayed away. During his individual time with the psychotherapist and key worker some more of his story unfolded, including the memory of being dressed and treated as a girl in his early years and suffering sexual abuse from various adults. What precipitated his move to England was never clear to us and this was probably the case for Steven himself. On the whole his recollections of his earlier life were vague and he seemed to be living in a mist of uncertainty and confusion about where he had come from and who he really was.

ALLEGATION AND ENDINGS

Steven's relationship with his original key worker remained a close one and contributed a good deal to the stability of his placement. Then, out of the blue, Steven made an allegation that Max (the key worker's name) had sexually abused him in his bedroom; "touching me up and trying to feel me" was how he described it. Of course, this added another dimension to the task of trying to contain and work creatively with Steven's presence in the community. Formal child protection procedures had to be implemented which included Max's suspension without prejudice, a series of statutory strategy meetings and the investigation into the allegation. Max completely denied the allegation and was both astounded that it had happened and frightened at its implications. At this stage Steven was quietly adamant that what he was saying was true.

Feelings within the community, amongst both staff and young people, raged fiercely between shock at what had happened to Max, fury towards Steven for making the allegation and fear that the allegation might be true. There was also an anxiety that LTC was perhaps not the safe place the young people especially hoped it would be and for some a sense of anger that dreadful and abusive things were 'happening to me' again. There were calls either for Steven to be immediately 'kicked out' or for Max to be sacked. Again the task was to try and contain the maelstrom of feelings; to ensure the procedures were followed but at the same time to give support to both Steven and Max and to the rest of the community. The whole life of the community became fixed around the events following the allegation, detracting from other business and deflecting work away from other sensitive and important areas concerning the young people. In the end, after several weeks of turmoil, with the investigation heading towards the usual inconclusive findings of no substantiating evidence, Steven withdrew the allegation, admitting he had made it up in order to "get at Max".

Max's confidence was shot to pieces and he refused to work with Steven, which given the circumstances was probably the safe option for both, although some reparative work would have been useful. Steven became more and more unsettled after the allegation and stayed on the receiving end of some pretty torrid abuse from other young people for quite some time. It was difficult to achieve any balance in either staff or community meetings about why Steven might have made the allegation or to accept the ambivalence of the feelings whirling around the community.

A PERSONAL REFLECTION

Over the next few months it became clear that Steven was looking to move on; we tried to think about to what extent this was due to the follow-on from the allegation, to the pressure Steven was under from the young people and unconsciously probably from the staff as well. However, in discussion with various workers from his local authority social work team, including those from the Independent Living scheme, it became clear that there was support for the idea of Steven leaving LTC. Once a final decision had been made there was undoubtedly a sense of relief amongst the wider community. The usual farewell rituals were observed including the purchase of a present and the organising of a party. It was a difficult time as most people seemed uncertain as to how they should feel or what was appropriate to say.

For me the experience of Steven brought into keen focus the purpose of the LTC and the difficulties involved in trying to stay faithful in practice to a set of principles and ideas when under extreme examination. Without question, maintaining the routine of the daily life of the community, keeping thinking alive, holding on when everything seemed about to explode and above all trusting in the relationships that we had worked hard to establish within the staff group and with the young people were the anchors that held the ship stable through the stormy waters we were passing through. Although it was necessary to ensure that we observed protocols and procedures, certainly during the child protection investigation, it was the strength of the human qualities that we shared that kept things together rather than a set of rules or procedures. These qualities included a sense of humour, compassion, thinking and reflecting rather than rushing into actions, trusting our judgements, being open and honest and above all trying to listen to each other and keep the whole story in mind as life went on and events occurred around us.

HOW NURTURE PROTECTS CHILDREN

The above case studies illustrate many of the points made in this book, although in the narrative they may appear in a different guise or be expressed in a different voice. Despite his many difficulties, it seems as if Richard did manage to find enough in his relationship with John and Helen to help him make the important transition to becoming an 'independent' adult and finding a way in the world, even if it feels unsatisfactory and incomplete. For Steven, it is likely that his whole life will continue to be a struggle. The hope is that the acceptance he found in the therapeutic community will remain with him and be a reminder in darker times that there are possibilities in human relationships for friendship and support.

In *How Nurture Protects Children*, I have tried to show the serious limitations and flaws in working with vulnerable children and young people when thinking and reflection are overwhelmed by bureaucratic protocols and procedures.

This bureaucracy occupies too much of our social workers, teachers and other professional workers' time, choking creativity and dangerously restricting the level of their direct contact with children and families. The culture of education courses and training programmes for the professional workforce has had to integrate the demands of the bureaucracy with the traditional expectations of higher education and this has created a set of worrying, longer-term problems. Even if it were possible to see some 'green shoots' indicating the beginnings of a shift away from rigid and formulaic practice, changing the wider culture of education and training and modifying the effects of what have been the dominant influences for so long will not be achieved overnight.

Relational approaches to all aspects of work with families, children and young people provide effective outcomes for disadvantaged and vulnerable people because they address their most deep-seated and real needs. 'Science' is now showing us how this is the case by clarifying and establishing the power of attachment relationships and the critical learning that takes place in the early years. This has become even better understood and supported by the growing knowledge and awareness that have come from studying human brain development through infancy and beyond.

To engage with people who are struggling in their lives, or with people whose behaviour is deviant or potentially violent towards themselves or others, is certain to create huge levels of anxiety. Learning to contain and manage this anxiety is an essential part of professional development for all workers. Of equal importance, however, workers must feel that they are free to practise their work in a management culture that understands, trusts and supports them, and that allows time for their work to progress and is not quick to blame if things go wrong. Of course, there has to be accountability; of course, there have to be high standards; and likewise, there have to be ways to demonstrate that what is happening is effective. It is, however, the ways in which these monitoring activities are carried out that matter, and these must be both consistent and appropriate to the nature of the task, and should give due weight to the lived experience of all the people involved.

Robert Frost's poem, *Birches* evokes a reflection about similarities between our work and life itself. What if, at times, the going seems hard and the feelings are unbearable? Perhaps we would just like to turn away and leave it all behind? But in the end we know that this is what we are and this is what we do and that *'Earth's the right place for love.'*

> *It's when I'm weary of considerations,*
> *And life is too much like a pathless wood*
> *Where your face burns and tickles with the cobwebs*
> *Broken across it, and one eye is weeping*
> *From a twig's having lashed across it open.*
> *I'd like to get away from earth awhile*
> *And then come back to it and begin over.*
> *May no fate wilfully misunderstand me*
> *And half grant what I wish and snatch me away*
> *Not to return. Earth's the right place for love:*
> *I don't know where it's likely to go better.*

(Robert Frost, *'Birches'*)

The qualities of creativity and imagination and the ability to trust experience and feelings may not be much valued for today's professional work force. They are, however, essential aspects of the whole raft of knowledge, experience and skills required to provide the policy and organisational context for practice built on the principles of nurture and which needy children, young people and families deserve. We scurry away from using the word 'love' in a professional context, but the importance of attachment and nurture as the basis for learning and healthy development surely draws us closer into an understanding of how relationships are central to all that we are and all that we do?

George Santayana wrote, *'It is wisdom to believe the heart';* perhaps we need more of that wisdom today? Or do we just need more of the heart?

REFERENCES AND SUGGESTIONS FOR FURTHER READING

Andrews, D. (2001) *'Vocational Professionals'*, Praxis Vol. 1.

Ayre, J. (1989) *Northrop Frye: A Biography*, London: Random House.

Beer, G. (2009) *Darwin's Plots*, Cambridge: C.U.P.

Bennathan, M. Boxall, M. (1998) *The Boxall Profile Handbook*, London: The Nurture Group Network.

—— (2000) *Effective Intervention in Primary Schools – Nurture Groups*. London: David Fulton Publishers

Bennathan, M. and Rose, J. (2008) *All About Nurture Groups*, London: The Nurture Group Network.

Bettelheim, B. (1950) *Love Is Not Enough,* New York: Glencoe Free Press.

Billington, T. (2000) *Separating, Losing and Excluding Children:* Narratives of Difference. London: Routledge Falmer.

—— (2006) *Working With Children,* London: Sage.

—— (2009) *'Working With Children: Psychologists at the Boundaries of Knowledge and Experience', The Psychology of Education Review,* Vol. 33, No 2, September 2009.

Bion, W. R. (1970) *Attention and Interpretation,* London: Tavistock Publications.

Blum, D. (2002) *Love at Goon Park,* Perseus: Columbia.

Blyth, M. Wright, C. and Newman, R. eds. (2008) *Children and Young People in Custody: Managing the Risk,* Bristol: The Policy Press

Boswell, G. (1995) *Violent Victims. The Prevalence of Abuse and Loss in the Lives of Section 53 Offenders,* London: The Prince's Trust.

Bourne, S. (2008) *Helping young offenders to learn,* Nurture, Issue 10, Summer 2008.

Bowlby, J. (1973) *Attachment and Loss, Vol. II: Separation, Anxiety and Anger,* London: Hogarth Press.

Boxall, M. (2002) *Nurture Groups in Schools – Principles & Practice,* London: Paul Chapman Publishing

Broadhurst, K. et al. (2009) *'Performing "Initial Assessment": Identifying the Latent Conditions for Error at the Front-Door of Local Authority Children's Services',* British Journal of Social Work 1–19.

Brown, D. Pedder, J. (1991) *Introduction to Psychotherapy,* London: Routledge.

Bullock, R., Little, M. and Millham, S. (1998) *Secure Treatment Outcomes,* Aldershot: Ashgate Publishing.

Clouder, C. Heyes, B. (2008) *'Aspects of Social and Emotional Learning in the United Kingdom',* An International Analysis of Social and Emotional Learning, Fundación Marcelino Botín.

Cooper, P., Whitebread, D. (2007) *'The Effectiveness of Nurture Groups on Student Progress: Evidence from a National Research Study',* Emotional and Behavioural Difficulties, 12:3, 171–190.

Cox, M. (1998) 'A Supervisor's View', in C. Cordess and M. Cox (eds) Forensic Psychotherapy, London and Philadelphia: Jessica Kingsley Publishers.

Cummins, A. (2002) 'Quality Assurance as a Social Defence Against Anxiety', Organisational and Social Dynamics 2(1).

Doctor, R. (2004) 'Assessing and Managing Risk: Psychodynamic Aspects', Forensische Psychiatrie und Psychotherapie Werkstattscriften, Lengerich: PABST Publishers

Eliot, T. S. (1968) 'Burnt Norton', Four Quartets, London: Faber and Faber.

Erikson, E. (1965) Childhood and Society, Harmondsworth: Penguin.

Etzioni, A. (1961) A Comparative Analysis of Complex Organisations, New York: Glencoe Free Press.

Fogerty, T.J. (1996) The Imagery and the Reality of Peer Review: Insights from Institutional Theory, Accounting, Organisation and Society, 21(2/3):243–267.

Freud, A. (1946) The Psycho-analytic Treatment of Children, London: Imago.

Gabriel, Y. (2000) Storytelling in Organisations: Facts, Fictions, and Fantasies, Oxford: O.U.P.

Garland, D. (2001) The Culture of Control, Oxford: O.U.P.

Geddes, H. (2006) Attachment in the Classroom, London: Worth Publishing Ltd.

Gill, T. (2007) No Fear: Growing up in a Risk Averse Society London: Caloustie Gulbenkian Foundation.

Goodwin, B. (1994) How the Leopard Changed Its Spots, London: Weidenfield and Nicholson.

Gopnik, A. (2009) Angels and Ages, London: Quercus.

Greenson, R.R. (1967) The Technique and Practise of Psychoanalysis, London: Hogarth Press.

Gregory, M. Holloway, M. (2005) Language and the Shaping of Social Work, BJSW Vol.35 No.1

Grotberg, E. (1995) 'A Guide to Promoting Resilience in Children: Strengthening the Human Spirit, The International Resilience Project', Early Childhood Development: Practice and Reflections series, Bernard Van Leer Foundation.

Handy, C. (1978) Gods of Management, London: Souvenir Press Ltd.

Henggeler, S. (1999) 'Multisystemic Therapy: An Overview of Clinical Procedures, Outcomes and Policy Implications', Child Psychology and Psychiatry Review, Vol.4 no.1 1999.

Hinshelwood, R. D. (1999) 'Psychoanalytic Origins and Today's Work: The Cassel Heritage', in P. Campling and R. Haigh (eds), Therapeutic Communities; Past, Present and Future, London: Jessica Kingsley Publishers.

Howe, D., Brandon. M., Hinings, D. and Schofield, G. (1999) Attachment Theory, Child Maltreatment and Family Support, London: Macmillan.

Hughes, L. and Pengelly, P. (1997) Staff Supervision in a Turbulent Environment, London: Jessica Kingsley Publishers.

Hutton, J., Bazalgette, J. and Armstrong, D. (1994) 'What Does Management

Really Mean?', in Casemore, R. et al. What Makes Consultancy Work – Understanding the Dynamics, London: Southbank University Press.

Jeffs, T., Spence, J. (2007/08) *'Farewell to all that? The uncertain future of youth and community work education',* Youth and Policy, Nos. 97 and 98, 135–166.

Kalisch, D. (1990) *'Professionalisation – A Rebel View',* Self and Society, Vol. 18 No 1. January 1990.

Keats., J. *Letters of John Keats.* R. Gittings, (ed.) Oxford: Oxford University Press. 1987.

Kets de Vries, M. (1980) *Organisational Paradoxes: Clinical Approaches to Management,* London: Tavistock.

Kraybill, D & Pellman Good, P (ed) (1982) *Perils of Professionalism,* Scottdale: Herald Press:

Lec, S. J, (1965) *Unkempt Thoughts,* Minerva Press

Likert and Likert, (1976) *New Ways of Managing Conflict,* Maidenhead: McGraw-Hill.

Lyon, J., Dennison, C. And Wilson, A. (2000) *'Tell Them So They Listen': Messages from Young People in Custody,* London: Home Office.

Menzies Lyth, I. (1959) *'The Functions of Social Systems as a Defence Against Anxiety: A Report on a Study of the Nursing Service of a General Hospital',* Human Relations 13: 95–121.

Mintzberg, H. (1973) *The Nature of Managerial Work,* New York: Harper & Row.

Morgan, A. (2000) *What is Narrative Therapy? An Easy to Read Introduction,* Adelaide, Australia: Dulwich Centre Publications

Palmer. P.J. (1998) *The Courage to Teach,* San Francisco: Jossey Bass

Pascale, R., Athos, A. (1981) *The Art of Japanese Management,* New York: Simm & Schuster.

Redl, F. (1966) *When We Deal With Children,* New York: The Free Press.

Redl, F. and Wineman, D. (1965) *Controls From Within,* New York: The Free Press.

Reynolds, S., MacKay, T., Kearney, M. (2009) *'Nurture groups: a large-scale, controlled study of effects on development and academic attainment'* British Journal of Special Education (in press).

Rhodes, C. (1996) *'Researching Organisational Change and Learning: A Narrative Approach'* The Qualitative Report, Vol. 2, Number 4.

Rose, J. (2002) *Working with Young People in Secure Accommodation - From Chaos to Culture,* London: Brunner – Routledge

—— (2004) *'It's the stories that matter',* Young Minds Magazine, November 2004

Rutter, M., Giller, H. and Hagell, A. (1998) *Antisocial Behaviour by Young People,* Cambridge: Cambridge University Press.

Rutty J. (1998) *'The nature of philosophy of science, theory and knowledge relating to nursing and professionalism',* Journal of Advanced Nursing. Vol. 28 No.2 pp 243–250.

Sameroff and Emde (eds.) (1989) *'The Infant's Relationship Experience: Developmental and Affective Aspects'*, *Relationship Disturbances in Early Childhood*, New York: Basic Books.

Shakespeare, *Macbeth* (Act II sc.5), Penguin (1979).

Sunderland, M. (2007) *What Every Parent Needs to Know*, London: DK.

Untermeyer, L. (1971) *Robert Frost's Poems*, New York: Washington Square Press.

White, M. (2007) *Maps of Narrative Practice*, New York: W.W. Norton.

Winnicott, D.W. (1956) *'The antisocial tendency', in D.W. Winnicott Collected Papers: Through Paediatrics to Psycho-analysis*, London: Tavistock.

Yalom, I. (1989) *Love's Executioner and Other Tales of Psychotherapy*, New York: Basic Books.

—— (1998) *The Yalom Reader*, New York: Basic Books.

Young, R. (1995) *'Mental Space and Group Relations'*, paper presented at seminar on Group Relations and Organisational Behaviour, New Bulgarian University.

REPORTS

DCSF (2009) *Building a safe, confident future*, the final report of the Social Work Task Force.

DCSF Report RR023 (2008) *'Analysing Child Deaths and Serious Injury Through Abuse and Neglect'*, The Department for Children Schools and Families Research Report on Serious Case Reviews.

Fish J. (1985), John Fish Report: *'Educational Opportunities for All?'* (London: ILEA).

Goldman, D. Cook, R. (2008) *Making our Experience Count:* Messages from Evaluation Studies. London: The Nurture Group Network.

Laming, Lord (2003) *'The Victoria Climbié Inquiry: Report of an Inquiry by Lord Laming'*.

Ofsted (2009) *'The exclusion of children from school of children aged four to Seven'*. www.ofsted.gov.uk/The-exclusion-from-school-of-children-aged-four-toseven

Overview & Scrutiny report (2009), *'Who Cares? Protecting Children and Improving Children's Social Care'*. Birmingham City Council, 13th October 2009,

Steer Report (2004, 2009) 'Learning Behaviour: A review of behaviour standards and practices in our schools' (see www.teachemet.gov.uk/publications. Ref DCSF-004532009).

The Children's Society (2008) *'A Good Childhood'*, report by The Children's Society. (2008) www.childrenssociety.org.uk

The Fostering Network (2008) *'What it means to be a professional foster carer'* www.fostering.net

The Warnock Report: *Special Educational Needs (1978)* London: HMSO.

The WAVE Report (2005) *'Violence and what to do about it'*.

OTHER

'A Talk with Brian Goodwin', A New Science of Qualities, www.edge.org (29.04.1997).

Avraamidou, L. And Osborne, J. (2008) 'Science as Narrative: The story of the discovery of penicillin', The Pantaneto Forum, Issue 31: July 2008 www.pantaneto.co.uk/issue31/front31.htm

Balbernie, R. (2007) 'Attachment Matters' PowerPoint presentation at SEBDA London Conference, May 2007.

Call of Story, website: www.callofstory.org

Document (1998) 'Meeting Special Educational Needs: A Programme of Action' London: DfEE.

Document (1999) Social Inclusion: Pupil Support DfES Circular 10/99.

Overview & Scrutiny report (2009), 'Who Cares? Protecting Children and Improving Children's Social Care'. Birmingham City Council, 13th October 2009, Mental Health Foundation: website: www.mentalhealth.org.uk/our-work/children-and-young-people

Stanford Encyclopaedia of Philosophy (2008) http://plato.stanford.edu

The Caspari Foundation: www.caspari.org

The Department for Children, Schools and Families. For information about SEAL and the Targeted Mental Health pilot in schools project see www.dcsf.gov.uk

The Nurture Group Network: www.nurturegroups.org

Wikipedia, information explosion: http://en.wikipedia.org/wiki/Information_explosion

Index